GRADE 3

Mathematics

Intervention Activities

Table of Contents

i

Using Mathematics Intervention Activities

Current research indicates that literacy activities that engage students in familiar, real-world math situations are essential for math skill development. The Mathematics Intervention Activities series offers activities that are carefully crafted to help students grow in language and literacy while acquiring core grade-level math content.

Effective mathematics activities provide students with opportunities to:

- Strengthen the language and literacy skills needed to develop math proficiency

- Relate math concepts to real-life situations

- Develop math computation and application skills

Although some students master these skills easily during regular classroom instruction, many others need additional reteaching opportunities to master these essential skills. The Mathematics Intervention Activities series provides easy-to-use, five-day intervention units for Grades K–5. These units are structured around a research-based Model-Guide-Practice-Apply approach and align with National Council of Teachers of Mathematics (NCTM) Focal Points and Common Core standards. You can use these activities in a variety of intervention models, including Response to Intervention (RTI).

Getting Started

In just five simple steps, Mathematics Intervention Activities provides everything you need to identify students' needs and to provide targeted intervention.

1. PRE-ASSESS to identify students'
mathematics needs. Use the pre-assessment to identify the skills your students need to master.

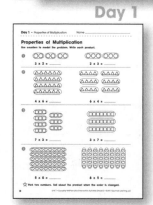

2. MODEL the skill.
Every five-day unit targets a specific mathematics area. On Day 1, use the teacher prompts and reproducible activity page to introduce and model the skill.

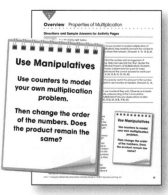

Day 1

3. GUIDE, PRACTICE, and APPLY.
Use the reproducible practice activities for Days 2, 3, and 4 to build students' understanding and skill proficiency.

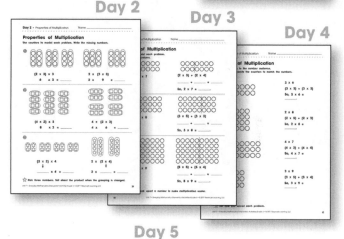

Day 2 **Day 3** **Day 4**

4. MONITOR progress.
Administer the Day 5 reproducible assessment to monitor each student's progress and to make instructional decisions.

Day 5

5. POST-ASSESS to document student progress.
Use the post-assessment to measure students' progress as a result of your interventions.

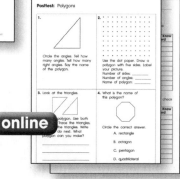

Standards-Based Mathematics Awareness Skills in Intervention Activities

The mathematics strategies found in the Intervention Activities series are introduced developmentally and spiral from one grade to the next. The chart below shows the types of skill areas addressed at each grade level in this series.

Mathematics Intervention Activities Series Skills	K	1	2	3	4	5
Counting & Cardinality	✔					
Number & Operations	✔	✔	✔	✔	✔	✔
Algebraic Thinking	✔	✔	✔	✔	✔	✔
Fractions				✔	✔	✔
Measurement & Data	✔	✔	✔	✔	✔	✔
Geometry	✔	✔	✔	✔	✔	✔

Using Intervention for RTI

According to the National Center on Response to Intervention, RTI "integrates assessment and intervention within a multi-level prevention system to maximize student achievement and to reduce behavior problems." This model of instruction and assessment allows schools to identify at-risk students, monitor their progress, provide research-proven interventions, and "adjust the intensity and nature of those interventions depending on a student's responsiveness."

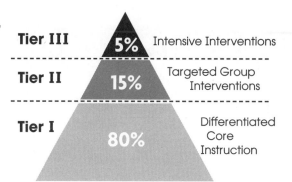

RTI models vary from district to district, but the most prevalent model is a three-tiered approach to instruction and assessment.

The Three Tiers of RTI	Using Intervention Activities
Tier I: Differentiated Core Instruction • Designed for all students • Preventive, proactive, standards-aligned instruction • Whole- and small-group differentiated instruction • Sixty-minute, daily core math instruction in the essential skill areas	• Use whole-group math mini-lessons to introduce and guide practice with math strategies that all students need to learn. • Use any or all of the units in the order that supports your core instructional program.
Tier II: Targeted Group Interventions • For struggling students • Provide thirty minutes of daily instruction beyond the sixty-minute Tier I core math instruction • Instruction is conducted in small groups of three to five students with similar needs	• Select units based on your students' areas of need (the pre-assessment can help you identify these). • Use the units as week-long, small-group mini-lessons.
Tier III: Intensive Interventions • For high-risk students experiencing considerable difficulty in mathematics • Provide up to sixty minutes of additional intensive intervention each day in addition to the sixty-minute Tier I core math instruction • More intense and explicit instruction • Instruction conducted individually or with smaller groups of one to three students with similar needs	• Select units based on your students' areas of need. • Use the units as one component of an intensive math intervention program.

Overview Use Place Value to Round Whole Numbers

Directions and Sample Answers for Activity Pages

Day 1	See "Model the Skill" below.
Day 2	Read the directions aloud. Remind students to locate the number on the number line to determine which hundred it is closer to. Have students check their work by looking at the tens digit to determine whether the hundreds place remains the same or if it should increase by one. (Answers: **1.** 200; **2.** 800; **3.** 500; **4.** 800)
Day 3	Read the directions aloud, pointing out that there are two answers for each problem. Suggest that students use their understanding of place value and the number lines to determine each rounded number. (Answers: **1.** 240, 200; **2.** 390, 400; **3.** 700, 700)
Day 4	Read the directions aloud. Point out that students must record three different numbers each time. Help students see that there are more than three possible answers for each problem. (Answers will vary. Possible answers: **1.** 28, 29, 31; **2.** 66, 68, 72; **3.** 95, 97, 104; **4.** 351, 389, 449)
Day 5	Read the directions aloud. Observe as students complete the page. Do students use understanding of place value to round numbers to the nearest ten or hundred? Do they round up when the digit to the right of the rounding place is 5? Use your observations to plan further instruction and review. (Answers: **1.** 80; **2.** 240; **3.** 400; **4.** answers will vary; possible answers: 452, 502, 545)

Model the Skill

◆ Hand out the Day 1 activity page.

◆ **Ask:** *How can you use a number line to help you round numbers?* (Locate the number on the line and see which ten or hundred it is closer to.) Invite students to circle 42 in problem 1 on the number line and determine which ten it is closer to. (40)

◆ **Say:** *You can also round numbers to the nearest ten by looking at the ones digits.* **Ask:** *What digit is in the ones place of 42?* (2) *How does that help you round 42?* (If the digit is less than 5, the tens digit stays the same. If it is 5 or greater, the tens digit increases by one.)

◆ Help students complete the activity page by using the number line to round each number to the nearest ten. Have them also explain how to round the same number just by looking at the ones digit. (Answers: **2.** 70; **3.** 330; **4.** 100)

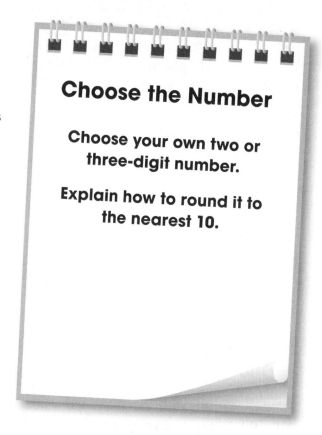

Choose the Number

Choose your own two or three-digit number.

Explain how to round it to the nearest 10.

Use Place Value to Round Whole Numbers

Use the number line. Round each number to the nearest ten.

①

42 _____

②

65 _____

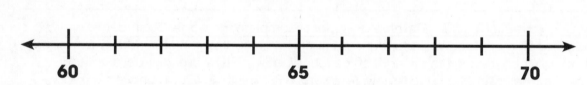

③

329 _____

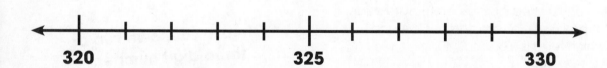

④

104 _____

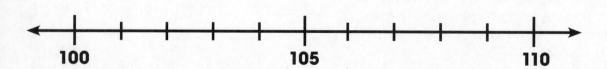

☆ **Tell** how to use a number line to round numbers to the nearest ten.

Use Place Value to Round Whole Numbers

Use the number line. Round each number to the nearest hundred.

1 234 _____

200   **250**   **300**

2 817 _____

800   **850**   **900**

3 453 _____

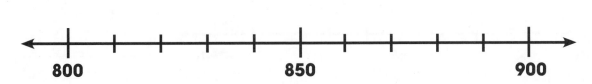

400   **450**   **500**

4 795 _____

700   **750**   **800**

☆ **Tell** how you can use a number line to round numbers to the nearest hundred.

Use Place Value to Round Whole Numbers

Round each number to the nearest ten and then the nearest hundred.

1

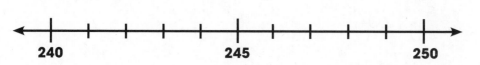

nearest ten

_____

243

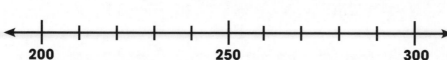

nearest hundred

_____

2

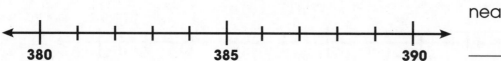

nearest ten

_____

386

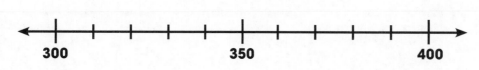

nearest hundred

_____

3

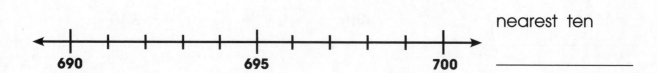

nearest ten

_____

698

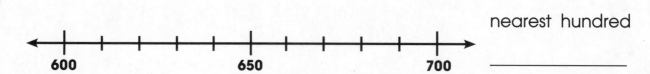

nearest hundred

_____

☆ **Tell how rounding to the nearest ten is similar to rounding to the nearest hundred.**

Use Place Value to Round Whole Numbers

Write three numbers that round to 30 when rounded to the nearest ten.

_____   _____   _____

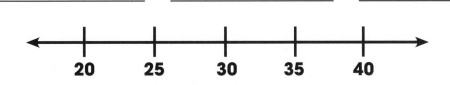

Write three numbers that round to 70 when rounded to the nearest ten.

_____   _____   _____

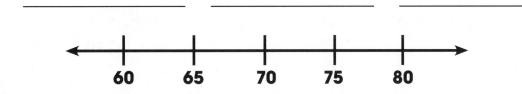

Write three numbers that round to 100 when rounded to the nearest hundred.

_____   _____   _____

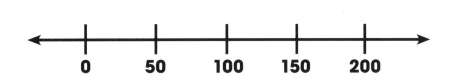

Write three numbers that round to 400 when rounded to the nearest hundred.

_____   _____   _____

⭐ **Tell how to use place value to round to the nearest ten or hundred.**

Assessment

Round each number to the nearest ten.

1   82 _____

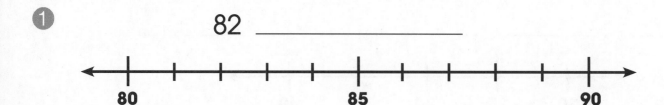

2   235 _____

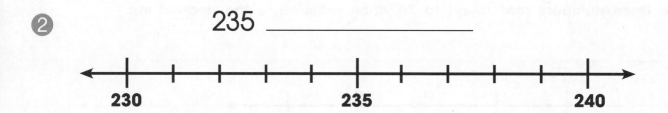

3 **Round to the nearest hundred.**

357 _____

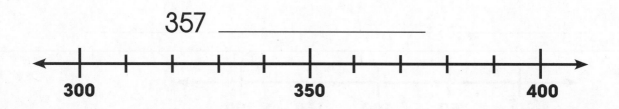

3 **Write three numbers that round to 500 when rounded to the nearest hundred.**

_____   _____   _____

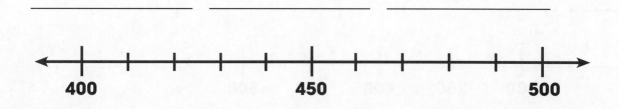

☆ **Tell why the numbers round to 500.**

     Unit 1 • Mathematics Intervention Activities Grade 3 • © 2014 Newmark Learning, LLC

Overview Estimate Sums and Differences

Directions and Sample Answers for Activity Pages

Day 1	See "Model the Skill" below.
Day 2	Read the directions aloud. Observe how students estimate. Do they round each addend or do they use mental math strategies, such as compatible numbers? Encourage students to share the strategies they use and explain why they chose a particular strategy. If rounding, students may choose to round addends to the nearest ten or hundred. (Answers will vary. Possible answers: **1.** 500; **2.** 600; **3.** 300; **4.** 900)
Day 3	Read the directions aloud. Remind students to record the rounded numbers to the right of the arrows and then find the difference. (Answers: **1.** 60 – 30 = 30; **2.** 50 – 30 = 20; **3.** 70 – 50 = 20; **4.** 90 – 30 = 60)
Day 4	Read the directions aloud. Observe whether students use rounding or mental math strategies to estimate each difference. Encourage students to share the strategies they use and explain why they chose a particular strategy. If rounding, students may choose to round to the nearest ten or hundred. (Answers will vary. Possible answers: **1.** 200; **2.** 300; **3.** 250; **4.** 600)
Day 5	Read the directions aloud. Students may find it necessary to find each estimated sum or difference in order to choose the problem that answers the question. Observe as students complete the page. Are they using rounding or mental math to estimate? Are they rounding to the nearest 10 or 100? Use your observations to plan further instruction and review. (Answers: **1.** 37 + 52; **2.** 435 + 416; **3.** 61 – 23; **4.** 764 – 153)

Model the Skill

◆ Hand out the Day 1 activity page.

◆ **Say:** *Today we are going to estimate sums and differences. A sum is the total when you add. A difference is the amount that is left when you subtract. Look at the page.* **Ask:** *Will you round the addends to the nearest ten or nearest hundred? Why?* (Answer: ten because the addends are much less than 100)

◆ **Ask:** *How can you use rounding to estimate the sum of 23 and 38?* (Round 23 to 20 and 38 to 40. Then add 20 and 40 to get 60.) *Why might rounding numbers to the nearest ten make it easier to add?* (Possible answer: It is easy to add tens.)

◆ Help students complete the activity page by rounding each addend to the nearest ten. Have them explain how they rounded each addend. (Answers: **2.** 40 + 40 = 80; **3.** 30 + 30 = 60; **4.** 70 + 20 = 90)

Use Manipulatives

Use base-ten blocks to model estimating the sum of two 2-digit numbers. Remove the ones models from numbers where there are four or fewer ones. If there are five or more ones, remove the ones and add one ten. Then count the tens to find the estimated sum.

Estimate Sums and Differences

Round each number. Then estimate the sum.

1

23 →

+ 38 →

+

2

41 →

+ 37 →

+

3

26 →

+ 28 →

+

4

72 →

+ 15 →

+

⭐ **Tell how you rounded each number.**

Estimate Sums and Differences

**Estimate each sum. Use rounding or mental math.
Show or write how you estimated.**

①
$$302$$
$$+\ 204$$

②
$$323$$
$$+\ 267$$

③
$$192$$
$$+\ \ 95$$

④
$$286$$
$$+\ 579$$

☆ **Tell how you estimated each sum.**

Estimate Sums and Differences

Round each number. Then estimate the difference.

1

$$62 \rightarrow$$
$$- \ 31 \rightarrow$$

2

$$46 \rightarrow$$
$$- \ 25 \rightarrow$$

3

$$67 \rightarrow$$
$$- \ 53 \rightarrow$$

4

$$85 \rightarrow$$
$$- \ 32 \rightarrow$$

☆ **Tell how you rounded each number.**

Estimate Sums and Differences

Estimate each difference. Use rounding or mental math.
Show or write how you estimated.

$$394 \rightarrow$$
$$- 193 \rightarrow$$

$$509 \rightarrow$$
$$- 206 \rightarrow$$

③

$$284 \rightarrow$$
$$- 29 \rightarrow$$

④

$$895 \rightarrow$$
$$- 259 \rightarrow$$

☆ **Tell how you estimated each difference.**

Assessment

1 Circle the problem that has a sum of about 90.

31	37	108
+ 28	+ 52	+ 81

2 Circle the problem that has a sum of about 800.

256	703	435
+ 307	+ 225	+ 416

3 Circle the problem that has a difference of about 40.

24	61	84
− 18	− 23	− 32

4 Circle the problem that has a difference of about 600.

764	432	775
− 153	− 187	− 314

☆ **Tell how you solved each problem.**

Overview   Add Whole Numbers

Directions and Sample Answers for Activity Pages

Day 1	See "Model the Skill" below.
Day 2	Read the directions aloud. Observe if students use place-value understanding to add two- and three-digit numbers. Help them with regrouping and recording as necessary. (Answers: **1.** 369; **2.** 235; **3.** 123; **4.** 205) Ask students how they know their answer to problem 4 is reasonable. (Possible response: You can estimate. 50 + 50 = 100, so the sum must be about 200.)
Day 3	Read the directions aloud. Draw a base-ten model for the numbers in problem 1 and help students connect the model to the place-value chart. Invite students to share their answers. (Answers: **1.** 368; **2.** 975; **3.** 762; **4.** 627) Ask students to explain how they add.
Day 4	Read the directions aloud. Observe whether students add hundreds first or ones first. Help them record regrouped numbers across 0 and regroup twice. (Answers: **1.** 341; **2.** 633; **3.** 700; **4.** 901) Ask students how they know their answer to problem 4 is reasonable. (Possible response: You can estimate. 396 is almost 400, so the sum must be about 900.)
Day 5	Read the directions aloud. Allow students to use base-ten blocks if they wish. Observe as students complete the page. Do students use place-value understanding to add and to regroup? Use your observations to plan further instruction and review. (Answers: **1.** 61; **2.** 207; **3.** 129; **4.** 476)

Model the Skill

◆ Hand out the Day 1 activity page.

◆ **Say:** *We are going to add today. We are going to find the sum. A sum is the total amount. Look at the models of tens and ones in the first problem. How many ones are there in all?* (6) Allow students to count or add the ones. Record the ones in the vertical addition.

◆ **Ask:** *How many tens are there in all?* (5) Record the tens. **Ask:** *What is the sum of 24 + 32?* (56) Help students connect the models to the standard algorithm by adding the ones first. Accept other ways to find the sum. Observe as students complete problem 2. (67)

◆ **Say:** *Now look at problem 3. What happens when you add the ones?* Students should recognize that 16 ones can be regrouped as 1 ten and 6 ones. Discuss how to record the regrouped ten. **Ask:** *How many tens are there in all?* (5) *What is the sum?* (56)

◆ Help students complete problem 4 with regrouping in the tens place. Allow students to use manipulatives as necessary. Ask students to explain how they add. (104)

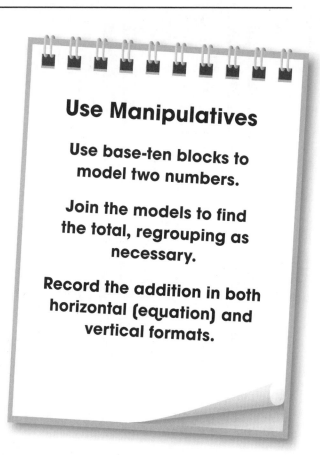

Use Manipulatives

Use base-ten blocks to model two numbers.

Join the models to find the total, regrouping as necessary.

Record the addition in both horizontal (equation) and vertical formats.

Add Whole Numbers

Find the sum for each problem.

①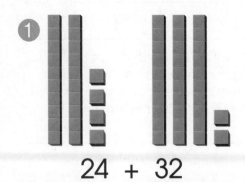

$$\begin{array}{r} 24 \\ +\ 32 \\ \hline \end{array}$$

24 + 32

②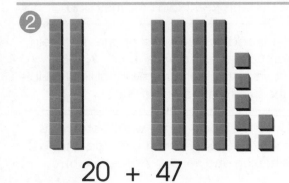

$$\begin{array}{r} 20 \\ +\ 47 \\ \hline \end{array}$$

20 + 47

③

$$\begin{array}{r} 28 \\ +\ 28 \\ \hline \end{array}$$

28 + 28

④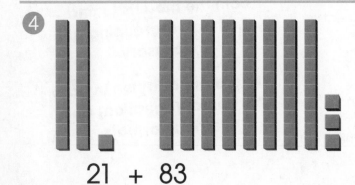

$$\begin{array}{r} 21 \\ +\ 83 \\ \hline \end{array}$$

21 + 83

☆ **Tell** how you add.

Add Whole Numbers

Find the sum for each problem.

①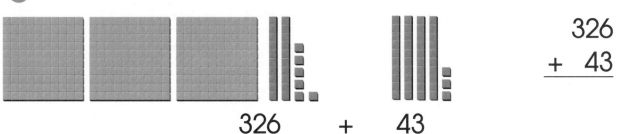

$$
\begin{array}{r}
326 \\
+\ \ 43 \\
\hline
\end{array}
$$

326 + 43

②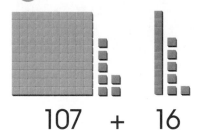

$$
\begin{array}{r}
200 \\
+\ \ 35 \\
\hline
\end{array}
$$

200 + 35

③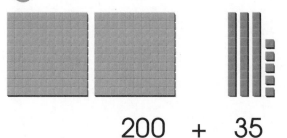

$$
\begin{array}{r}
107 \\
+\ \ 16 \\
\hline
\end{array}
$$

107 + 16

④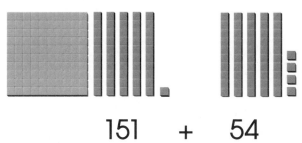

$$
\begin{array}{r}
151 \\
+\ \ 54 \\
\hline
\end{array}
$$

151 + 54

☆ **Tell how you know your answer is reasonable.**

Name _____

Add Whole Numbers

Find the sum for each problem.

1   246 + 122

hundreds	tens	ones
2	4	6
+ 1	2	2

2   300 + 675

hundreds	tens	ones
3	0	0
+ 6	7	5

3   546 + 216

hundreds	tens	ones
5	4	6
+ 2	1	6

4   492 + 135

hundreds	tens	ones
4	9	2
+ 1	3	5

☆ **Tell how you add.**

Add Whole Numbers

Find the sum for each problem.

1   207 + 134

hundreds	tens	ones
2	0	7
+ 1	3	4

2   386 + 247

hundreds	tens	ones
3	8	6
+ 2	4	7

3   265 + 435

hundreds	tens	ones
2	6	5
+ 4	3	5

4   396 + 505

hundreds	tens	ones
3	9	6
+ 5	0	5

☆ **Tell how you know your answer is reasonable.**

Assessment

Solve each problem. Show your work.

 1

$$27 + 34$$

$$\begin{array}{r} 27 \\ +\ 34 \\ \hline \end{array}$$

---

2    $62 + 145$

hundreds	tens	ones
	6	2
+ 1	4	5

---

3    $53 + 76$

hundreds	tens	ones
	5	3
+	7	6

---

4    $238 + 238$

hundreds	tens	ones
2	3	8
+ 2	3	8

☆ **Tell how you solved each problem.**

Overview   Subtract Whole Numbers

Directions and Sample Answers for Activity Pages

Day 1	See "Model the Skill" below.
Day 2	Read the directions aloud. Observe if students use place-value understanding to subtract two- and three-digit numbers. Help them with regrouping and recording as necessary. Suggest students use models or cross out and draw additional models to show regrouping. (Answers: **1.** 215; **2.** 136; **3.** 324; **4.** 363) Ask students how they know their answer to problem 4 is reasonable. (Possible response: You can estimate. 400 – 50 = 350; 363 is close to 350.)
Day 3	Read the directions aloud. Draw a base-ten model for the numbers in problem 1 and help students connect the model to the place-value chart. Invite students to share their answers. Allow students to use base-ten blocks if they wish. (Answers: **1.** 116; **2.** 255; **3.** 346; **4.** 391)
Day 4	Read the directions aloud. Observe whether students subtract hundreds first or ones first. Help them record regrouped numbers and regroup twice. (Answers: **1.** 217; **2.** 109; **3.** 487; **4.** 288) Ask students how they know their answer to problem 4 is reasonable. (Possible response: You can estimate. 550 – 250 = 300; 288 is close to 300.)
Day 5	Read the directions aloud. Allow students to use base-ten blocks if they wish. Observe as students complete the page. Do students use place-value understanding to subtract and to regroup? Can they solve problem 5 using the standard algorithm? Use your observations to plan further instruction and review. (Answers: **1.** 47; **2.** 59; **3.** 501; **4.** 279; **5.** 311)

Model the Skill

◆ Hand out the Day 1 activity page.

◆ **Say:** *We are going to subtract today. We are going to find the difference. Look at the models of tens and ones in the first problem. How many ones are there?* (5) *How many ones are you going to take away?* (2) Allow students to cross out 2 ones and record the difference.

◆ **Ask:** *How many tens are there?* (3) *How many tens are you going to take away?* (1) Allow students to cross out 1 ten and record the remaining tens. (2) **Ask:** *What is the difference of 35 – 12?* (23) Help students connect the models to the standard algorithm by subtracting the ones first. Observe as students complete problem 2. (16)

◆ **Say:** *Look at problem 3. What happens when you subtract the ones?* Students should recognize that there are not enough ones to subtract and therefore they must regroup. Discuss how to regroup and record the regrouped ten. **Ask:** *How many ones and tens are left after subtracting?* (9 ones, 3 tens) *What is the difference?* (39)

◆ Help students complete problem 4. Allow them to use manipulatives as necessary. (47)

Use Manipulatives

Use base-ten blocks to model a two-digit subtraction problem.

Take away the models to find the difference, regrouping as necessary.

Record the subtraction in both horizontal (equation) and vertical formats.

Subtract Whole Numbers

Find the difference for each problem.

1

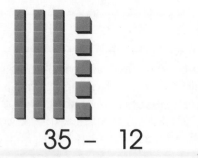

$$35 - 12$$

$$\begin{array}{r} 35 \\ -\ 12 \\ \hline \end{array}$$

2

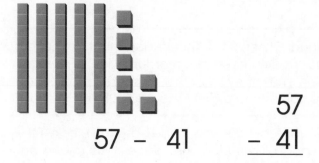

$$57 - 41$$

$$\begin{array}{r} 57 \\ -\ 41 \\ \hline \end{array}$$

3

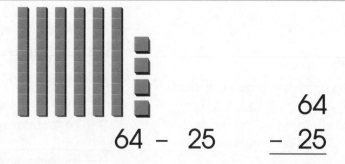

$$64 - 25$$

$$\begin{array}{r} 64 \\ -\ 25 \\ \hline \end{array}$$

4

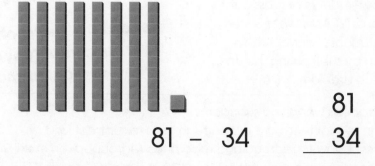

$$81 - 34$$

$$\begin{array}{r} 81 \\ -\ 34 \\ \hline \end{array}$$

☆ **Tell how you subtract.**

Subtract Whole Numbers

Find the difference for each problem.

①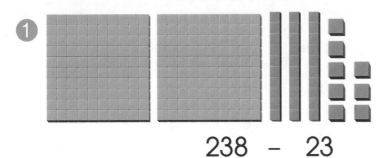

238 – 23

$\begin{array}{r} 238 \\ -\ 23 \\ \hline \end{array}$

②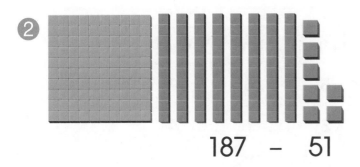

187 – 51

$\begin{array}{r} 187 \\ -\ 51 \\ \hline \end{array}$

③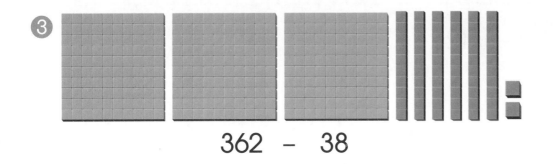

362 – 38

$\begin{array}{r} 362 \\ -\ 38 \\ \hline \end{array}$

④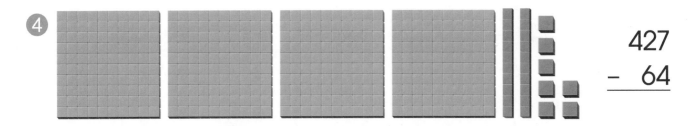

427 – 64

$\begin{array}{r} 427 \\ -\ 64 \\ \hline \end{array}$

⭐ **Tell how you know your answer is reasonable.**

Name _____

Subtract Whole Numbers

Find the difference for each problem.

1   347 – 231

hundreds	tens	ones
3	4	7
- 2	3	1

2   569 – 314

hundreds	tens	ones
5	6	9
- 3	1	4

3   475 – 129

hundreds	tens	ones
4	7	5
- 1	2	9

4   684 – 293

hundreds	tens	ones
6	8	4
- 2	9	3

☆ **Tell how you subtract.**

Subtract Whole Numbers

Find the difference for each problem.

1   632 – 415

hundreds	tens	ones
6	3	2
– 4	1	5

2   318 – 209

hundreds	tens	ones
3	1	8
– 2	0	9

3   876 – 389

hundreds	tens	ones
8	7	6
– 3	8	9

4   567 – 279

hundreds	tens	ones
5	6	7
– 2	7	9

☆ **Tell how you know your answer is reasonable.**

Assessment

Solve each problem. Show your work.

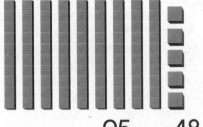

$$95 - 48 = ?$$

$$\begin{array}{r} 95 \\ -\ 48 \\ \hline \end{array}$$

$$136 - 77 = ?$$

hundreds	tens	ones
1	3	6
−	7	7

$$670 - 169 = ?$$

hundreds	tens	ones
6	7	0
− 1	6	9

$$452 - 173 = ?$$

hundreds	tens	ones
4	5	2
− 1	7	3

$$708 - 397 = ?$$

_____

☆ **Tell how you solved the problem.**

Overview Solve Two-Step Problems

Directions and Sample Answers for Activity Pages

Day 1	See "Model the Skill" below.
Day 2	Read the directions aloud. Tell students that each problem on the page takes two steps to solve. Help students identify the given information and the letter that represents the unknown quantity in each problem. Encourage students to assess the reasonableness of their answers. (Answers: **1.** 9, 9, 9; **2.** 7, 7, 7; **3.** 4, 4, 4; **4.** 8, 8, 8)
Day 3	Read the directions aloud. Remind students that any letter can be used to represent an unknown quantity. In this case, the letter *n* is used in each number sentence (equation). Point out that the unknown quantity can appear in any part of the number sentence. (Answers: **1.** 12 − 5 − n = 4, 3, 3; **2.** 6 + 5 + n = 16, 5, 5; **3.** 16 − 5 − 2 = n, 9, 9; **4.** n + 7 + 3 = 18, 8, 8)
Day 4	Read the directions aloud. Tell students to use a letter to represent the number they do not know. Observe whether they record the number sentence correctly. Allow students to use counters to model the problem if they wish. (Possible answers: **1.** 3 + 4 + 6 = n, 13; **2.** 11 = 3 + 3 + n, 5; **3.** n + 6 + 5 = 20, 9; **4.** 8 + 7 − 3 = n, 12)
Day 5	Read the directions aloud. Allow students to use counters if they wish. Observe as students complete the page. Do they represent each problem with an equation including a letter standing for the unknown quantity? Use your observations to plan further instruction and review. (Possible answers: **1.** 8 + 7 + 8 = n, 23; **2.** 15 = 7 + 4 + n, 4; **3.** 12 − n + 9 = 16, 5; **4.** 24 = 9 + 5 + n, 10)

Model the Skill

◆ Hand out the Day 1 activity page.

◆ **Say:** *Today we are going to solve problems that use a letter to stand for an unknown quantity. Look at problem 1.* **Ask:** *What do we know?* (Sam has 3 apples and some bananas. He has 8 pieces of fruit in all.) *What do we need to find out?* (how many bananas Sam has) *What letter should we use to represent the number of bananas?* (b) Point out that any letter can be used to represent an unknown quantity.

◆ Using red counters, model the apples. Ask a volunteer to add yellow counters to make a total of 8. **Say:** *How many apples are there?* (3) *How many bananas did we add to make 8 pieces of fruit in all?* (5) *How many counters are there in all?* (8)

◆ Have students complete problems 2–4, identifying the letter that stands for each unknown quantity. Help students complete the activity by recording the value of the unknown quantity and the answer to the problem in the given space. Suggest that students use counters of two colors if they wish. (Answers: **2.** 9, 9, 9; **3.** 48, 48, 48; **4.** 10, 10, 10)

Use Manipulatives

Use counters to model an addition or subtraction problem with an unknown quantity.

Record the addition or subtraction sentence.

Solve Two-Step Problems

Write the missing numbers.

1 Sam has 3 apples.
He has some bananas.

He has 8 pieces of fruit in all.

How many bananas **(b)** does Sam have?

3 + b = 8

3 + _____ = 8

b = _____

Sam has _____ bananas.

2 Tomas baked 16 cookies.
He gave some to his aunt.

He has 7 cookies left.

How many cookies **(c)** did Tomas give to his aunt?

16 - c = 7

16 - _____ = 7

c = _____

Tomas gave _____ cookies to his aunt.

3 Ana read 12 pages of a book.

She has 36 more pages to read.

How many pages are in the book **(p)**?

12 + 36 = p

12 + 36 = _____

p = _____

There are _____ pages in the book.

4 Dana has some football cards and 27 baseball cards.

She has 37 sports cards in all.

How many football cards **(f)** does she have?

f + 27 = 37

_____ + 27 = 37

f = _____

Dana has _____ football cards.

⭐ **Tell how you found the missing number.**

Solve Two-Step Problems

Write the missing numbers.

1 Lily bakes 8 muffins.
She bakes 4 more.
She gives 3 muffins to her friends.

How many muffins **(m)** does she have now?

$8 + 4 - 3 = m$

$8 + 4 - 3 =$ _____

$m =$ _____

Lily has _____ muffins now.

2 Ms. Green picked vegetables from her garden.
She picked some tomatoes, 7 carrots, and 5 peppers.
She picked 19 vegetables in all.

How many tomatoes **(t)** did she pick?

$t + 7 + 5 = 19$

_____ $+ 7 + 5 = 19$

$t =$ _____

Ms. Green picked _____ tomatoes.

3 Ramon has 15 model cars.
He has 6 red cars, some white cars, and 5 black cars.

How many white cars **(w)** does he have?

$6 + w + 5 = 15$

$6 +$ _____ $+ 5 = 15$

$w =$ _____

Ramon has _____ white cards.

4 Mia had 16 photos in her scrapbook.
She took out 6 of the photos.
Then she put in some new photos.
Now there are 18 photos in the book.

How many new photos **(n)** did she put in the book?

$16 - 6 + n = 18$

$16 - 6 +$ _____ $= 18$

$n =$ _____

Mia put _____ new photos in her scrapbook.

⭐ **Tell how you found the missing numbers.**

Name _____

Solve Two-Step Problems

Match the problem to the number sentence you can
use to solve it. Then solve the problem.

$n + 7 + 3 = 18$

① Lucy had 12 apples. She gave 5 to Eric
and some to Sue. She has 4 apples left.

How many apples did she give to Sue?

n = _____

Lucy gave _____ apples to Sue.

$16 - 5 - 2 = n$

② Ramon read 6 pages of a book on
Monday. He read 5 pages on Tuesday.
He read the rest of the book on Wednesday.
There are 16 pages in the book.

How many pages did he read on
Wednesday?

n = _____

Ramon read _____ pages on Wednesday.

$12 - 5 - n = 4$

③ Jorge's baseball team played 16 games.
The team lost 5 games and tied 2 games.
How many games did the team win?

n = _____

The team won _____ games.

$6 + 5 + n = 16$

④ Ali has some blue pens. She has 7 black
pens and 3 red pens. She has 18 pens
in all.

How many blue pens does she have?

n = _____

Ali has _____ blue pens.

⭐ **Tell how each number sentence matches the problem.**

  Unit 5 • Mathematics Intervention Activities Grade 3 • © 2014 Newmark Learning, LLC

Solve Two-Step Problems

**Write a number sentence to solve the problem.
Then solve the problem.**

① There are 3 apples, 4 pears, and 6 bananas in a fruit bowl.

How many pieces of fruit are in the bowl?

_____ + _____ + _____ = n

There are _____ pieces of fruit in the bowl.

② Marie runs 11 miles in three days.

She runs 3 miles on each of the first two days.

How many miles does she run on the third day?

_____ = _____ + _____ + n

Marie runs _____ miles on the third day.

③ Kit has some green balloons, 6 yellow balloons, and 5 blue balloons.

She has 20 balloons in all.

How many green balloons (n) does she have?

n + _____ + _____ = 20

Kit has _____ green balloons.

④ Evan baked 8 bran muffins and 7 blueberry muffins.

He gave 3 of his muffins to a friend.

How many muffins (n) does Evan have left?

_____ + _____ − _____ = n

Evan has _____ muffins left.

⭐ **Tell how each number sentence matches the problem.**

Assessment

**Write a number sentence to solve the problem.
Then solve the problem.**

1 A vase is filled with flowers.

There are 8 lilies, 7 roses, and 8 daisies.

How many flowers are in the vase?

_____ + _____ + _____ = n

_____ flowers

2 Debbie has 15 stamps.

She put 7 stamps on one page of her stamp book.

She put 4 stamps on another page of her book.

How many stamps did she NOT use?

15 = _____ + _____ + n

_____ stamps

3 Alex picks 12 grapes.

He eats some of them and then picks 9 more.

He has 16 grapes now.

How many grapes did he eat?

_____ **- n + 9 = 16**

_____ grapes

4 Kim has a box of 24 crayons.

She has 9 crayons in the box and 5 crayons on her desk.

The rest of them are in her desk.

How many crayons are in her desk?

24 = _____ + _____ + n

_____ crayons

⭐ **Tell how the number sentence matches the problem.**

 Unit 5 • Mathematics Intervention Activities Grade 3 • © 2014 Newmark Learning, LLC

Overview Meaning of Multiplication

Directions and Sample Answers for Activity Pages

Day 1	See "Model the Skill" below.
Day 2	Read the directions aloud. Observe if students understand that the sum and the product are the same. (Answers: **1.** 12, 3, 4, 12; **2.** 18, 3, 6, 18; **3.** 16, 2, 8, 16; **4.** 20, 5, 4, 20) Help them see how the addition sentence is related to the multiplication sentence.
Day 3	Read the directions aloud. Remind students that the answer to an addition problem is called the sum and the answer to a multiplication problem is called the product. (Answers: **1.** 10; **2.** 21; **3.** 24; **4.** 20)
Day 4	Read the directions aloud. Allow students to use counters to model the problem before recording the number sentences. (Answers: **1.** 4 + 4 = 8, 2 x 4 = 8; **2.** 3 + 3 + 3 = 9, 3 x 3 = 9; **3.** 2 + 2 + 2 + 2 + 2 + 2 + 2 + 2 = 16, 8 x 2 = 16; **4.** 3 + 3 + 3 + 3 + 3 = 15, 5 x 3 = 15)
Day 5	Read the directions aloud. Allow students to model each problem with counters if they wish. Observe as students complete the page. Do they recognize that the sum and product must be the same? Do they record the correct number of addends in problems 3 and 4? Do they use the operation signs correctly? Use your observations to plan further instruction and review. (Answers: **1.** 6, 3, 2, 6; **2.** 16, 4, 4, 16; **3.** 6 + 6 + 6 + 6 + 6 = 30, 5 x 6 = 30; **4.** 7 + 7 + 7 = 21, 3 x 7 = 21)

Model the Skill

◆ Hand out the Day 1 activity page and distribute counters.

◆ **Say:** *We are going to see how addition and multiplication are related.* Have students use counters to model 4 groups of 3.

◆ **Ask:** *How many equal groups are there in problem 1?* (4) *How many counters are there in each group?* (3) *How many counters are there in all?* (12)

◆ **Say:** *You can record 4 groups of 3 as an addition sentence or as a multiplication sentence.* Have students record the sum and the product. **Ask:** *What is the sum of 3 + 3 + 3 + 3?* (12) *What is the product of 4 x 3?* (12) *Remember, to multiply you need equal groups.*

◆ Help students complete the activity page by modeling the problem and recording each sum and product. (Answers: **2.** 10, 10; **3.** 12, 12; **4.** 15, 15)

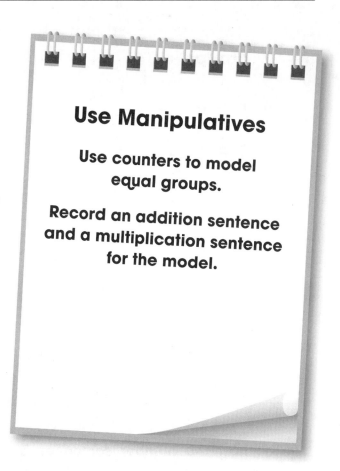

Use Manipulatives

Use counters to model equal groups.

Record an addition sentence and a multiplication sentence for the model.

Name _____

Meaning of Multiplication

Use counters to model the problem. Draw a picture to show your work. Complete each number sentence.

① **4 groups of 3**

$$3 + 3 + 3 + 3 = \text{_____}$$

$$4 \times 3 = \text{_____}$$

② **5 groups of 2**

$$2 + 2 + 2 + 2 + 2 = \text{_____}$$

$$5 \times 2 = \text{_____}$$

③ **2 groups of 6**

$$6 + 6 = \text{_____}$$

$$2 \times 6 = \text{_____}$$

④ **3 groups of 5**

$$5 + 5 + 5 = \text{_____}$$

$$3 \times 5 = \text{_____}$$

 **Tell how the number sentences both describe your picture.**

Unit 6 • Mathematics Intervention Activities Grade 3 • © 2014 Newmark Learning, LLC

Meaning of Multiplication

Write the missing numbers.

① 4 + 4 + 4 = _____

_____ groups of _____

3 x 4 = _____

② 6 + 6 + 6 = _____

_____ groups of _____

3 x 6 = _____

③ 8 + 8 = _____

_____ groups of _____

2 x 8 = _____

④ 4 + 4 + 4 + 4 + 4 = _____

_____ groups of _____

5 x 4 = _____

☆ **Tell** how the addition sentence and the multiplication sentence are the same.

Meaning of Multiplication

Draw a picture for each multiplication sentence. Describe the picture. Then find the product.

1   **5 x 2 = _____**

_____

_____

2   **3 x 7 = _____**

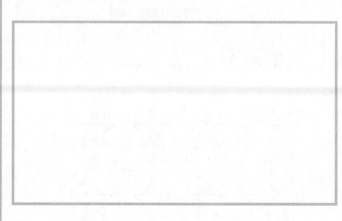

_____

_____

3   **6 x 4 = _____**

_____

4   **4 x 5 = _____**

_____

 Tell how you found the product.

Meaning of Multiplication

Write an addition sentence and a multiplication sentence for each picture.

①

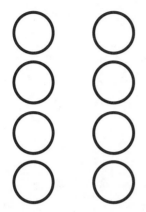

_____

_____

②

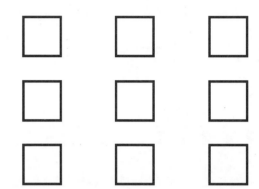

_____

_____

③

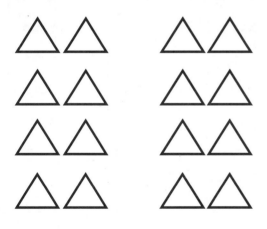

_____

④

_____

☆ **Tell how both number sentences describe the picture.**

Assessment

Write the missing numbers.

①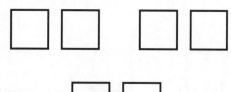

2 + 2 + 2 = _____

_____ groups of _____

3 x 2 = _____

② (array of circles: 4 rows × 4 columns)

4 + 4 + 4 + 4 = _____

_____ groups of _____

4 x 4 = _____

Write an addition sentence and a multiplication sentence for each picture.

③
(triangles: 5 rows of 6)

_____

_____

④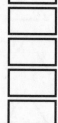
(three columns of squares)

_____

_____

⭐ **Tell** how multiplication is similar to adding equal groups.

Overview   Properties of Multiplication

Directions and Sample Answers for Activity Pages

Day 1	See "Model the Skill" below.
Day 2	Read the directions aloud. Demonstrate how to use counters to model multiplication of three numbers (Associative Property of Multiplication). Help students connect the models to the multiplication sentences. Invite students to share their answers. (Answers: **1.** 18, 18; **2.** 24, 24; **3.** 4, 16; 8, 16)
Day 3	Read the directions aloud. Help students see that the number and arrangement of counters in both parts of problem 1 are the same. Help them see that the "line" divides the counters into two simpler multiplications (Distributive Property of Multiplication). Students should see that in each problem the second factor is broken into two parts to make multiplication easier. Observe whether students record the correct answers for each part of the problem. (Answers: **1.** 6, 8, 14, 14; **2.** 15, 9, 24, 24; **3.** 25, 20, 45, 45)
Day 4	Read the directions aloud. Observe if students correctly match the pictures to the number expressions and sentences. Encourage students to use counters as needed. (Answers: **1.** 16; **2.** 28; **3.** 27; **4.** 18)
Day 5	Read the directions aloud. Allow students to use counters if they wish. Observe as students complete the page. Do students demonstrate understanding of the Commutative, Associative, and Distributive Properties of Multiplication? Use your observations to plan further instruction and review. (Answers: **1.** 20, 20 **2.** 30, 30 **3.** 18 **4.** 32)

Model the Skill

◆   Hand out the Day 1 activity page.

◆   Have students use counters to model the Commutative Property of Multiplication. **Say:** *Today we are going to multiply two numbers and then change the order of the numbers to see if the product will change.* Have students model along as you demonstrate how to show 3 x 2 with counters.

◆   **Ask:** *How many groups of counters are there? How many counters in each group? What is the product of 3 x 2?*

◆   **Say:** *Now let's see what happens to the product when we change the order of the numbers.* Guide students to model 2 x 3. **Ask:** *How many groups of counters are there? How many counters are there in each group? What is the product of 2 x 3? Does changing the order of the numbers change the product?* (No) **Say:** *If you know 3 x 2 = 6, then you know 2 x 3 = 6.*

◆   Observe students as they complete problems 2–4. Do they model each problem correctly? Do they recognize without modeling that the product for pairs of problems is the same? (Answers: **2.** 24, 24; **3.** 21, 21; **4.** 40, 40)

Use Manipulatives

Use counters to model your own multiplication problem.

Then change the order of the numbers. Does the product remain the same?

Properties of Multiplication

Use counters to model the problem. Write each product.

①

   3 x 2 = _____   2 x 3 = _____

②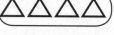

   4 x 6 = _____   6 x 4 = _____

③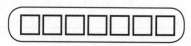

   7 x 3 = _____   3 x 7 = _____

④

   5 x 8 = _____   8 x 5 = _____

☆ **Pick two numbers. Tell about the product when the order is changed.**

Properties of Multiplication

Use counters to model each problem. Write the missing numbers.

 1

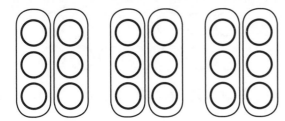 

(2 x 3) x 3   **2 x (3 x 3)**

6   x 3 = _____   **2 x   9   = _____**

 2

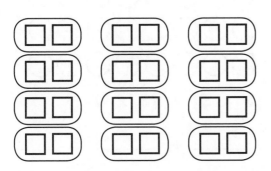 

(4 x 2) x 3   **4 x (2 x 3)**

8   x 3 = _____   **4 x   6   = _____**

3

(2 x 2) x 4   **2 x (2 x 4)**
↓   ↓

_____ x 4 = _____   **2 x _____ = _____**

⭐ **Pick three numbers. Tell about the product when the grouping is changed.**

Properties of Multiplication

Use counters to model each problem.
Write the missing numbers.

① ⭕⭕⭕⭕⭕⭕⭕
⭕⭕⭕⭕⭕⭕⭕

2 x 7

⭕⭕⭕|⭕⭕⭕⭕
⭕⭕⭕|⭕⭕⭕⭕

(2 x 3) + (2 x 4)

_____ + _____ = _____

So, 2 x 7 = _____.

② ⭕⭕⭕⭕⭕⭕⭕⭕
⭕⭕⭕⭕⭕⭕⭕⭕
⭕⭕⭕⭕⭕⭕⭕⭕

3 x 8

⭕⭕⭕⭕⭕|⭕⭕⭕
⭕⭕⭕⭕⭕|⭕⭕⭕
⭕⭕⭕⭕⭕|⭕⭕⭕

(3 x 5) + (3 x 3)

_____ + _____ = _____

So, 3 x 8 = _____.

③ ⭕⭕⭕⭕⭕⭕⭕⭕⭕
⭕⭕⭕⭕⭕⭕⭕⭕⭕
⭕⭕⭕⭕⭕⭕⭕⭕⭕
⭕⭕⭕⭕⭕⭕⭕⭕⭕
⭕⭕⭕⭕⭕⭕⭕⭕⭕

5 x 9

⭕⭕⭕⭕⭕|⭕⭕⭕⭕
⭕⭕⭕⭕⭕|⭕⭕⭕⭕
⭕⭕⭕⭕⭕|⭕⭕⭕⭕
⭕⭕⭕⭕⭕|⭕⭕⭕⭕
⭕⭕⭕⭕⭕|⭕⭕⭕⭕

(5 x 5) + (5 x 4)

_____ + _____ = _____

So, 5 x 9 = _____.

⭐ **Tell how to break apart a number to make multiplication easier.**

Unit 7 • Mathematics Intervention Activities Grade 3 • © 2014 Newmark Learning, LLC

Properties of Multiplication

Connect the counters to the correct number sentence.
Then draw lines to separate the counters to match the numbers.

1

3 x 6

(3 x 3) + (3 x 3)

So, 3 x 6 =

_____.

2

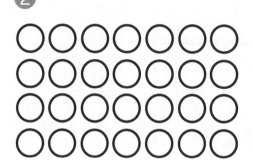

2 x 8

(2 x 5) + (2 x 3)

So, 2 x 8 =

_____.

3

4 x 7

(4 x 3) + (4 x 4)

So, 4 x 7 =

_____.

4

3 x 9

(3 x 5) + (3 x 4)

So, 3 x 9 =

_____.

☆ **Tell how you solved each problem.**

Assessment

Find the product.

5 x 4 = _____   4 x 5 = _____

 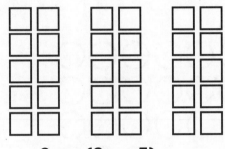

(3 x 2) x 5   3 x (2 x 5)

6 x 5 = _____   3 x 10 = _____

**Draw a line to separate the counters to match the numbers.
Write the product.**

③ **2 x 9**

    (2 x 5) + (2 x 4)

    So, 2 x 9 = _____ .

④ **4 x 8**

    (4 x 4) + (4 x 4)

    So, 4 x 8 = _____ .

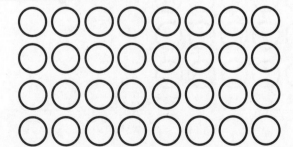

⭐ **Tell how you solved each problem.**

Overview Patterns in Multiplication

Directions and Sample Answers for Activity Pages

Day 1	See "Model the Skill" below.
Day 2	Read the directions aloud. Demonstrate how to use the multiplication table. Help students record the missing numbers. Invite students to share their answers by stating a complete number sentence, such as "3 x 6 = 18." Encourage students to describe patterns they see within rows, columns, and diagonally.
Day 3	Read the directions aloud. Allow students to use counters if necessary. Observe if students record the correct answers in the correct places. (Answers: **1.** 8, 10; **2.** 10¢, 25¢; **3.** top row: 5; bottom row: 16, 20; **4.** top row: 4, 5; bottom row: 24, 30)
Day 4	Read the directions aloud. Have students draw jump marks over the number line in problem 4. Observe whether students use patterns to multiply by 10 and multiples of 10. (Answers: **1.** 30; **2.** 50; **3.** 80; **4.** 60)
Day 5	Read the directions aloud. Allow students to use counters if they wish. Observe as students complete the page. Do students use patterns to solve the problems? Use your observations to plan further instruction and review. (Answers: **1.** 8, **2.** 0; **3.** 12, 15 **3.** 60)

Model the Skill

◆ Hand out the Day 1 activity page.

◆ Have students use counters to model the first part of problem 1. **Say:** *Today we are going to look for patterns when we multiply by 1 and 0.* Have students model along as you demonstrate how to show 1 x 3 with counters.

◆ **Ask:** *How many groups of counters are there? How many counters are there in the group? What is the product of 1 x 3?*

◆ **Say:** *Now let's try the next part of problem 1.* **Ask:** *How many groups of counters are there? How many counters are there in each group? What is the product of 1 x 4?* Repeat for 1 x 5 and 1 x 6. (3, 4, 5, 6) **Say:** *What pattern do you see when we multiply with 1?* (Possible response: the product is always the other factor.)

◆ Follow a similar process for the first part of problem 2. **Ask:** *Why don't you need counters to model 0 x 3?* (Possible response: because there are 0 groups of 3 which means you don't need any counters.) Observe students as they complete problem 2. (0, 0, 0, 0) Do they recognize the pattern for multiplying with zero?

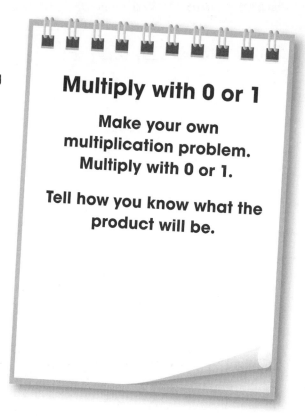

Multiply with 0 or 1

Make your own multiplication problem. Multiply with 0 or 1.

Tell how you know what the product will be.

Name _____

Patterns in Multiplication

Multiply with 1. Write each product.

① 1 x 3 = _____ ☆☆☆

1 x 4 = _____ ◯◯◯◯

1 x 5 = _____ ▢▢▢▢▢

1 x 6 = _____ ◇◇◇◇◇◇

Multiply with 0. Write each product.

② 0 x 3 = _____

0 x 4 = _____

0 x 5 = _____

0 x 6 = _____

☆ **Tell a rule to multiply with 0.**

Patterns in Multiplication

Complete the multiplication table.

Look for patterns.

x	0	1	2	3	4	5	6	7	8	9	10
0	0	0	0	0	0	0	0	0	0		
1	0	1	2	3	4	5	6	7			
2	0	2	4	6	8	10	12				20
3	0	3	6	9	12	15					
4	0	4	8	12	16						
5	0	5	10	15		25					50
6	0	6	12							54	
7	0	7		21							
8	0								64		
9							54				
10				30				70			100

☆ Tell about the patterns in the table.

Name _____

Patterns in Multiplication

Complete each table.
Look for patterns.

Number of Bicycles	1	2	3	4	5
Number of Wheels	2	4	6		

②

Number of Nickels	1	2	3	4	5
Value	5¢		15¢	20¢	

③

Number of Chairs	1	2	3	4	
Number of Legs	4	8	12		

④

Number of Insects	1	2	3		
Number of Legs	6	12	18		

☆ **Tell about the patterns in the table.**

 Unit 8 • Mathematics Intervention Activities Grade 3 • © 2014 Newmark Learning, LLC

Patterns in Multiplication

Find the product for each problem.

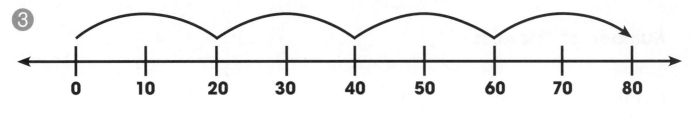

$3 \times 10 =$ _____

$5 \times 10 =$ _____

Use the number line. Find the product for each problem.

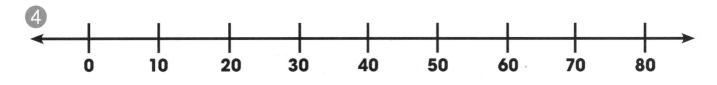

$4 \times 20 =$ _____

$2 \times 30 =$ _____

⭐ **Tell about a pattern when multiplying with tens.**

Assessment

Find the product for each problem.

1 x 8 = _____

0 x 9 = _____

③

Write the missing numbers in the table.

Number of Tricycles	1	2	3	4	5
Number of Wheels	3	6	9		

④

Use the number line. Find the product.

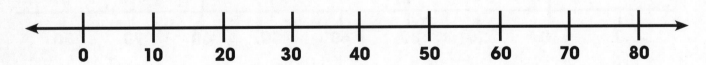

3 x 20 = _____

 Tell about a pattern when multiplying with tens.

Overview Meaning of Division

Directions and Sample Answers for Activity Pages

Day 1	See "Model the Skill" below.
Day 2	Read the directions aloud. Allow students to use counters to solve each problem. Have students identify the total number of counters each time. Tell students that each ring shows a group of counters. (Answers: **1.** 3, 3; **2.** 4, 4; **3.** 5, 6, 6; **4.** 32, 4, 8, 32 ÷ 4 = 8)
Day 3	Read the directions aloud. Have students first model the counters in each problem, then draw rings around counters in the picture to show the groups. (Answers: **1.** 2, 2; **2.** 6, 6; **3.** 2, 2; **4.** 5, 5)
Day 4	Read the directions aloud. Encourage students to use counters to model problems 3 and 4. (Answers: **1.** 16 ÷ 4 = 4; **2.** Possible answer: 18 ÷ 6 = 3; **3.** Possible answer: 8 ÷ 2 = 4; **4.** Possible answer: 12 ÷ 4 = 3)
Day 5	Read the directions aloud. Allow students to model each problem with counters if they wish. Observe as students complete the page. Can they identify the number of objects in each equal group? Can they identify the number of equal groups when a number of items is partitioned equally? Use your observations to plan further instruction and review. (Answers: **1.** 4, 0, 2; **2.** 7, 7; **3.** 4, 4; **4.** Possible answer: 24 ÷ 4 = 6)

Model the Skill

◆ Hand out the Day 1 activity page and distribute counters.

◆ Discuss how addition and multiplication are related. **Say:** *Today we will see how subtraction and division are related.* Have students use counters to model repeated subtraction of 2 in problem 1.

◆ **Ask:** *How may counters did you start with?* (8) *What number did you subtract each time? How many times did you subtract 2?* **Say:** *You subtracted 2 until you got an answer of zero. You subtracted 2 four times. You can say that there are 4 groups of 2 in 8.*

◆ Remind students that the answer to a division problem is called the quotient. Help students connect the repeated subtraction to the division sentence. **Ask:** *What is the quotient of 8 ÷ 2?* (4)

◆ Help students complete the activity page by modeling each subtraction problem and recording the missing numbers. Students should see that in each problem, they subtract the same number until they get 0 as the difference. (Answers: **1.** 6, 4, 2, 0, 4; **2.** 12, 9, 6, 3, 0, 5, 5; **3.** 4, 2, 0, 3; **4.** 15, 10, 5, 0, 4)

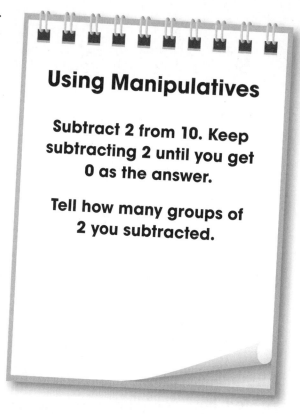

Using Manipulatives

Subtract 2 from 10. Keep subtracting 2 until you get 0 as the answer.

Tell how many groups of 2 you subtracted.

Name _____

Meaning of Division

**Use counters to model each subtraction.
Write the missing numbers.**

1 8 – 2 = _____

6 – 2 = _____

4 – 2 = _____

2 – 2 = _____

Subtract 2. Subtract 4 times.

8 ÷ 2 = _____

2 15 – 3 = _____

12 – 3 = _____

9 – 3 = _____

6 – 3 = _____

3 – 3 = _____

Subtract 3. Subtract _____ times.

15 ÷ 3 = _____

3 Subtract 2 until you get 0.

6 – 2 = _____

4 – 2 = _____

2 – 2 = _____

6 ÷ 2 = _____

4 Subtract 5 until you get 0.

20 – 5 = _____

15 – 5 = _____

10 – 5 = _____

5 – 5 = _____

20 ÷ 5 = _____

⭐ **Tell how you got your answers.**

Name _____

Meaning of Division

Write the missing numbers.

1

6 in all

2 equal groups

_____ in each group

6 ÷ 2 = _____

2

12 in all

3 equal groups

_____ in each group

12 ÷ 3 = _____

3

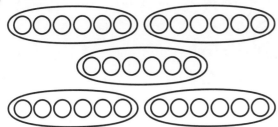

30 in all

_____ equal groups

_____ in each group

30 ÷ 5 = _____

4

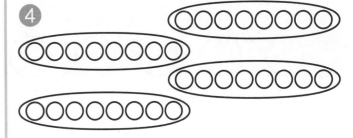

_____ in all

_____ equal groups

_____ in each group

_____ ÷ _____ = _____

⭐ **Tell what each number in the division sentence means.**

Meaning of Division

**Use counters to model the problem. Draw rings to show the groups.
Write the missing numbers**

1

4 in each group

_____ equal groups

8 ÷ 4 = _____

2

2 in each group

_____ equal groups

12 ÷ 2 = _____

3

3 equal groups

_____ in each group

6 ÷ 3 = _____

4

2 equal groups

_____ in each group

10 ÷ 2 = _____

☆ **Tell how you solved each problem.**

Meaning of Division

Write a division sentence for each problem.

1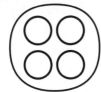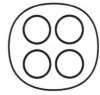

_____ ÷ _____ = _____

2

 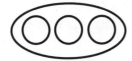 

_____ ÷ _____ = _____

Draw rings to show equal groups. Write the division sentence.

3

_____ ÷ _____ = _____

4

_____ ÷ _____ = _____

⭐ **Tell how to show equal groups another way.**

Assessment

Write the missing numbers.

1 8 − 4 = _____

4 − 4 = _____

8 ÷ 4 = _____

---

2 2 in each group

_____ equal groups

14 ÷ 2 = _____

Draw rings to show equal groups. Write the missing numbers.

3

3 equal groups

_____ in each group

12 ÷ 3 = _____

Write a division sentence for the picture.

4

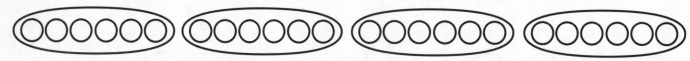

_____ ÷ _____ = _____

 Tell how the division sentence matches the picture.

Overview   Fact Families for Multiplication and Division

Directions and Sample Answers for Activity Pages

Day 1	See "Model the Skill" below.
Day 2	Read the directions aloud. Demonstrate how to model problem 1. Point out the rows and columns in the picture. Show how the counters can show 4 rows of 5, or 5 columns of 4. Help students complete each fact family. (Answers: **1.** 20, 4, 5; **2.** 24, 3, 8; **3.** 14, 2, 7; **4.** 6 x 4 = 24, 6, 24 ÷ 6 = 4)
Day 3	Read the directions aloud. Allow students to use counters if they wish. Have students identify the "members" of each fact family. (Answers: **1.** 3 x 8 = 24, 8 x 3 = 24, 24 ÷ 3 = 8, 24 ÷ 8 = 3; **2.** 3 x 6 = 18, 6 x 3 = 18, 18 ÷ 3 = 6, 18 ÷ 6 = 3; **3.** 2 x 9 = 18, 9 x 2 = 18, 18 ÷ 2 = 9, 18 ÷ 9 = 2; **4.** 7 x 6 = 42, 6 x 7 = 42, 42 ÷ 7 = 6, 42 ÷ 6 = 7)
Day 4	Read the directions aloud. Have students identify the fact family members in problems 1 and 2. Students should recognize that there are two multiplication and two related division sentences for each fact family on the page. Allow students to use counters if they wish. (Answers: **1.** 27, 9, 3; **2.** 35, 5, 7; **3.** 5 x 6 = 30, 6 x 5 = 30, 30 ÷ 5 = 6, 30 ÷ 6 = 5; **4.** 4 x 8 = 32, 8 x 4 = 32, 32 ÷ 4 = 8, 32 ÷ 8 = 4)
Day 5	Read the directions aloud. Allow students to model each problem with counters if they wish. Observe as students complete the page. Can they identify the missing number in each fact family regardless of its position? Do they recognize why there are only two number sentences for problem 4? Use your observations to plan further instruction and review. (Answers: **1.** 12, 6, 2; **2.** 20, 5, 4, 20; **3.** 5 x 8 = 40, 8 x 5 = 40, 40 ÷ 5 = 8, 40 ÷ 8 = 5; **4.** 4 x 4 = 16, 16 ÷ 4 = 4)

Model the Skill

◆ Hand out the Day 1 activity page and counters.

◆ **Say:** *Multiplication and division are opposite operations. That means they undo each other.* Demonstrate how to use counters to model 4 groups of 3 in problem 1. **Ask:** *How many groups of counters are there?* (4) *How many counters are in each group?* (3) *How many counters are there in all?* (12)

◆ Then demonstrate how to separate 12 counters into 4 equal groups. **Ask:** *How many counters did I start with?* (12) *How many groups did I make?* (4) *How many counters are there in each group?* (3) **Say:** *12 divided into 4 groups is 3 in each group.* Remind students that the answer to a division problem is called the quotient. Demonstrate how to record the quotient.

◆ Help students complete the activity page by modeling problem 2. Encourage them to use counters to match the multiplication problems to the related division problem in problems 3–6. (Answers: **2.** 6; **3.** 15 ÷ 3 = 5; **4.** 32 ÷ 4 = 8; **5.** 35 ÷ 7 = 5; **6.** 8 ÷ 4 = 2)

Using Manipulatives

Use counters to make equal groups. Find the total.

Tell a multiplication and division sentence for the equal groups of counters.

Fact Families for Multiplication and Division

Find the missing numbers.

1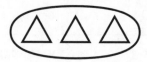

4 x 3 = 12

12 ÷ 4 = _____

2

5 x 6 = 30

30 ÷ 5 = _____

Match the multiplication sentence to the related division sentence. Then solve.

3   3 x 5 = 15   32 ÷ 4 = _____

4   4 x 8 = 32   35 ÷ 7 = _____

5   7 x 5 = 35   8 ÷ 4 = _____

6   4 x 2 = 8   15 ÷ 3 = _____

☆ **Tell how you got your answers.**

Fact Families for Multiplication and Division

Use counters. Complete each fact family.

1

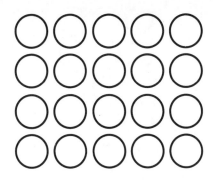

5 x 4 = 20

4 x 5 = _____

20 ÷ 5 = _____

20 ÷ 4 = _____

2

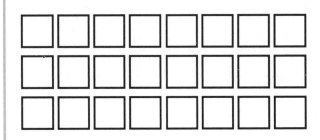

3 x 8 = 24

8 x 3 = _____

24 ÷ 8 = _____

24 ÷ 3 = _____

3

7 x 2 = 14

2 x 7 = _____

14 ÷ 7 = _____

14 ÷ 2 = _____

4

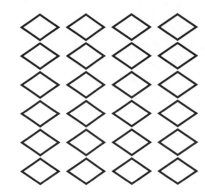

4 x 6 = 24

_____ x _____ = _____

24 ÷ 4 = _____

_____ ÷ _____ = _____

⭐ **Tell how you found the missing numbers.**

Fact Families for Multiplication and Division

Write a fact family for the picture.

1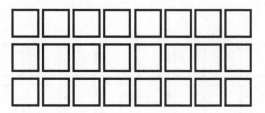

_____ X _____ = _____

_____ X _____ = _____

_____ ÷ _____ = _____

_____ ÷ _____ = _____

2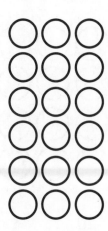

_____ X _____ = _____

_____ X _____ = _____

_____ ÷ _____ = _____

_____ ÷ _____ = _____

3

☆☆☆☆☆☆☆☆
☆☆☆☆☆☆☆☆

_____ X _____ = _____

_____ X _____ = _____

_____ ÷ _____ = _____

_____ ÷ _____ = _____

4

△△△△△△
△△△△△△
△△△△△△
△△△△△△
△△△△△△
△△△△△△
△△△△△△

_____ X _____ = _____

_____ X _____ = _____

_____ ÷ _____ = _____

_____ ÷ _____ = _____

☆ **Tell how the number sentences match the picture.**

Fact Families for Multiplication and Division

Complete each fact family.

1

$3 \times 9 = 27$

$9 \times 3 =$ _____

$27 \div 3 =$ _____

$27 \div 9 =$ _____

2

$7 \times 5 = 35$

$5 \times 7 =$ _____

$35 \div 7 =$ _____

$35 \div 5 =$ _____

Use the numbers to write a fact family.

3

5, 6, 30

_____ X _____ = _____

_____ X _____ = _____

_____ ÷ _____ = _____

_____ ÷ _____ = _____

4

4, 8, 32

_____ X _____ = _____

_____ X _____ = _____

_____ ÷ _____ = _____

_____ ÷ _____ = _____

☆ **Tell how to show equal groups another way.**

Assessment

Complete each fact family.

$2 \times 6 = 12$

$6 \times 2 =$ _____

$12 \div 2 =$ _____

$12 \div 6 =$ _____

②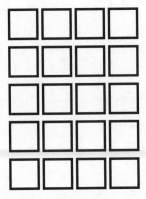

$5 \times 4 =$ _____

$4 \times$ _____ $= 20$

$20 \div 5 =$ _____

_____ $\div 4 = 5$

Use the numbers to write each fact family.

③

5, 8, 40

_____ $\times$ _____ $=$ _____

_____ $\times$ _____ $=$ _____

_____ $\div$ _____ $=$ _____

_____ $\div$ _____ $=$ _____

④

4, 4, 16

_____ $\times$ _____ $=$ _____

_____ $\div$ _____ $=$ _____

☆ **Tell why there are only two number sentences in this fact family.**

Overview Solve Multiplication and Division Problems

Directions and Sample Answers for Activity Pages

Day 1	See "Model the Skill" below.
Day 2	Read the directions aloud. Discuss how the pictures model problems 1–3. Encourage students to use counters to solve problem 4 if they wish. Help students see that each problem involves either finding the number of equal groups, or finding the number of items in each equal group. Have students share the strategies they use. (Answers: **1.** 3; **2.** 2; **3.** 5; **4.** 6)
Day 3	Read the directions aloud. Tell students that each picture is an array. Draw the array for problem 1 on the board and have students identify the rows and columns. Have students share their strategies for solving each problem. Ask how they could use multiplication to solve problems 1 and 3, and division to solve problems 2 and 4. Help them identify the total and the missing part that must be found each time. (Answers: **1.** 10; **2.** 6; **3.** 48; **4.** 5)
Day 4	Read the directions aloud. Tell students to first match the number sentence to the correct problem, complete the number sentence, then record the answer to the problem in the correct place. (Answers: **1.** 36 ÷ 9 = 4, 4; **2.** 6 x 9 = 54, 54; **3.** 42 ÷ 6 = 7, 7; **4.** 4 x 5 = 20, 20)
Day 5	Read the directions aloud. Allow students to model each problem with counters if they wish. Observe as students complete the page. How do they solve problems 1 and 2? Do they correctly divide and multiply to solve problems 3 and 4? Use your observations to plan further instruction and review. (Answers: **1.** 21; **2.** 8; **3.** 6, 6; **4.** 54, 54)

Model the Skill

◆ Hand out the Day 1 activity page.

◆ **Say:** *Today we are going to solve different types of word problems. Look at problem 1. How many flowers are there in each vase?* (3) *How many vases are there?* (5) *There are 5 groups of 3 flowers. How can we find how many flowers there are in all?* Have students share different strategies for finding the total number of flowers. (15; Possible responses: count the flowers; find the total of 5 groups of 3)

◆ Use counters to demonstrate how to use repeated addition and multiplication to solve the problem.
Say: *You can use repeated addition or multiplication to find the total number of flowers. The sum and the product will be the same.*

◆ Help students complete the activity page and share their strategies. Allow them to use counters if they wish. (Answers: **2.** 40; **3.** 12; **4.** 32)

Using Manipulatives

Tell a story about equal groups.

Use counters to model the story.

Name _____

Solve Multiplication and Division Problems

Solve each problem.

1 There are 3 flowers in each vase.
There are 5 vases.
How many flowers are there?

_____ flowers

2 There are 8 crayons in each box.
There are 5 boxes of crayons.
How many crayons are there?

_____ crayons

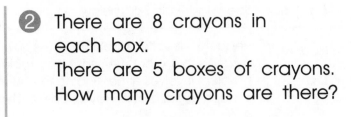

3 There are 4 rows of flowers.
There are 3 flowers in each row.
How many flowers are there?

_____ flowers

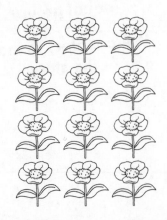

4 There are 4 rows of apples.
There are 8 apples in each row.
How many apples are there?

_____ apples

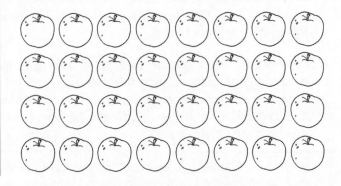

⭐ **Tell how you got your answers.**

Solve Multiplication and Division Problems

Solve each problem.

1 Sam has 15 apples.
He places an equal number of apples on each plate.
He has 5 plates.
How many apples does he put on each plate?

_____ apples

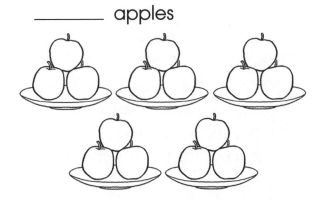

2 Jon has 10 books and some shelves.
He wants to place 5 books on each shelf.
How many shelves does he need?

_____ shelves

3 Tim plants 25 flowers in rows.
There are 5 flowers in each row.
How many rows of flowers are there?

_____ flowers

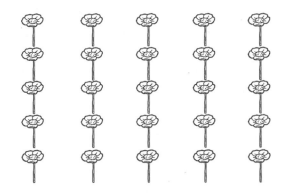

4 Ann places 18 muffins in 3 equal rows.
How many muffins are there in each row?

_____ muffins

⭐ **Tell how you solved the problem.**

Solve Multiplication and Division Problems

Use the array to solve each problem.

① 2 rows of 5

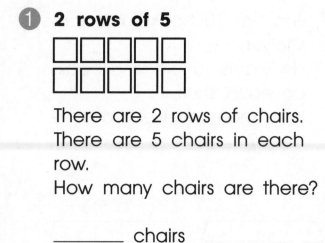

There are 2 rows of chairs.
There are 5 chairs in each row.
How many chairs are there?

_____ chairs

② 6 rows of 4

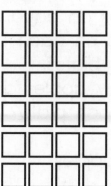

There are 24 plants in the garden. The plants are placed in equal rows. There are 4 plants in each row. How many rows of plants are there?

_____ rows

③ 6 rows of 8

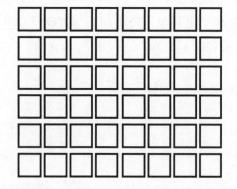

There are 6 rows of roses.
There are 8 roses in each row.
How many roses are there?

_____ roses

④ 5 rows of 9

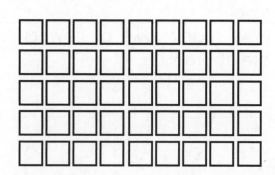

Mike plants 45 seeds in equal rows. He plants 9 seeds in each row. How many rows does he plant?

_____ rows

☆ **Tell how you know your answer is reasonable.**

Solve Multiplication and Division Problems

Match the problem to the number sentence. Use counters to solve.

1. Anita bakes 36 muffins.
   She put 9 muffins in each pan.
   How many pans does she use?   **4 x 5 = _____**

   _____ pans

2. Dan builds a wall with blocks.
   He puts 6 blocks in each row.
   He builds 9 rows.
   How many blocks does he use?   **42 ÷ 6 = _____**

   _____ blocks

3. Juan picked 42 apples. He put them
   in 6 baskets.
   He put the same number of apples
   in each basket.   **36 ÷ 9 = _____**
   How many apples did he put in
   each basket?

   _____ apples

4. Lil has 4 pens.
   She has 5 times as many crayons.   **6 x 9 = _____**
   How many crayons does she have?

   _____ crayons

⭐ **Tell how the number sentence matches the problem.**

Assessment

Solve each problem.

1 There are 3 flowers in each pot. There are 7 flower pots. How many flowers are there?

_____ flowers

2 There are 4 equal rows of chairs in a room. There are 32 chairs in all. How many chairs are in each row?

_____ chairs

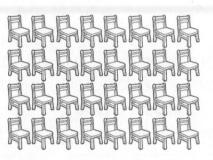

Complete the number sentence to solve each problem.

3 There are 30 desks in the classroom. There are 5 equal rows of desks. How many desks are there in each row?

30 ÷ 5 = _____

_____ desks

4 Brian has 6 stamps on each page of his stamp book. There are 9 pages in his book. How many stamps are in the book?

6 x 9 = _____

_____ stamps

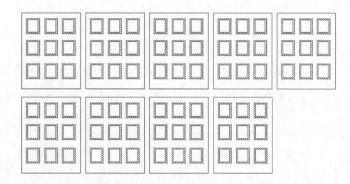

⭐ **Tell why you can use multiplication to solve the problem.**

Overview   Use Multiplication or Division to Find the Missing Number

Directions and Sample Answers for Activity Pages

Day 1	See "Model the Skill" below.
Day 2	Read the directions aloud. Help students identify which number is missing in each division sentence. Have them share the strategies they use to find the missing numbers. (Answers: **1.** 3; **2.** 4; **3.** 6; **4.** 30)
Day 3	Read the directions aloud. Tell students that the missing number may be part of a multiplication or division sentence. Demonstrate how they might think of a multiplication sentence to help them solve each problem. For example, for problem 1 they might think 4 x 2 = 8, so 8 ÷ 4 = 2. Have students share their strategies for solving each problem. (Answers: **1.** 2; **2.** 3; **3.** 5; **4.** 4)
Day 4	Read the directions aloud. Tell students that they can use a related multiplication fact to solve a division problem. Demonstrate how to use the array to complete the number sentences in problem 1. (Answers: **1.** 6, 6; **2.** 9, 9; **3.** 8, 8; **4.** 7, 7)
Day 5	Read the directions aloud. Allow students to model each problem with counters if they wish. Observe as students complete the page. Do they understand how to use related facts to solve multiplication and division problems? In problem 2, do they recognize that the quotient is on the left side of the equal sign? Use your observations to plan further instruction and review. (Answers: **1.** 8; **2.** 5; **3.** 3 x 4 = 12, 4; **4.** 4 x 9 = 36, 9)

Model the Skill

◆ Hand out the Day 1 activity page and distribute counters.

◆ **Say:** *Today we are going to model multiplication problems to find the missing product or factor.* Remind students that the factors are the numbers that are multiplied, and the product is the answer to the multiplication problem.

◆ Have students look at problem 1. **Ask:** *Is the product or a factor missing?* (product) *How do you know?* (Possible answer: The missing number is by itself after the equal sign.) *What are the factors?* (8 and 3) *How can you model the problem?* (Possible response: Show 8 groups of 3 counters) Have students model, record, and share their work. *What is the product?* (24)

◆ Have students look at problem 2. **Ask:** *Is the product or a factor missing?* (factor) *How do you know?* (Possible answer: The missing number comes right after the multiplication sign.) Have students model the problem with counters, then draw to record their work.

◆ Help students complete the activity page and share their strategies for finding the missing factors in problems 2–4. (Answers: **2.** 7; **3.** 4; **4.** 6)

Using Manipulatives

Use counters to make equal groups.

Tell a missing factor problem to match the counters.

Use Multiplication or Division to Find the Missing Number

Use counters to model the problem. Draw a picture to show your work. Complete each number sentence.

1

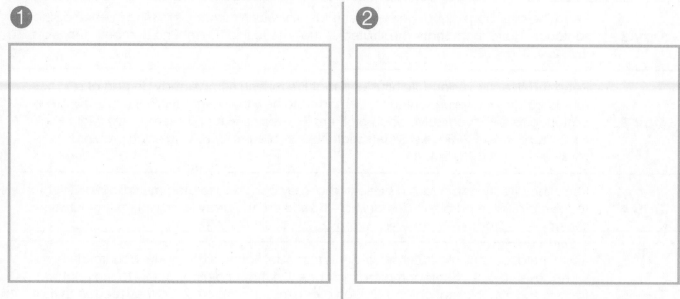

8 x 3 = _____

2

3 x _____ = 21

3

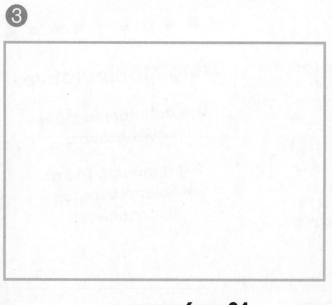

_____ x 6 = 24

4

7 x _____ = 42

☆ **Tell** how to use your picture to solve the problem.

Use Multiplication or Division to Find the Missing Number

**Use counters to model the problem.
Complete each number sentence.**

1

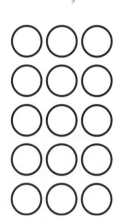

$$15 \div 5 = \underline{\hspace{2cm}}$$

2

$$12 \div \underline{\hspace{2cm}} = 3$$

3

$$42 \div \underline{\hspace{2cm}} = 7$$

4

$$\underline{\hspace{2cm}} \div 6 = 5$$

⭐ **Tell how you solved the problem.**

Use Multiplication or Division to Find the Missing Number

Use the array to solve each problem.

1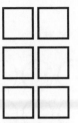

$8 \div 4 =$ _____

2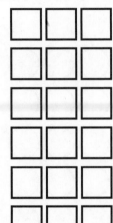

$6 \times$ _____ $= 18$

3

_____ $\times 8 = 40$

4

_____ $= 12 \div 3$

☆ **Tell how you solved each problem.**

Use Multiplication or Division to Find the Missing Number

Find the missing factor. Then use it to complete the division sentence.

1 **36 ÷ 6 = ?**

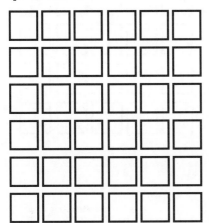

Think: 6 x _____ = 36

So, 36 ÷ 6 = _____.

2 **27 ÷ ? = 3**

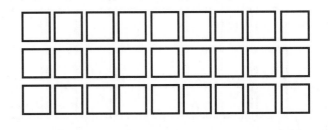

Think: 3 x _____ = 27

So, 27 ÷ _____ = 3.

3 **32 ÷ ? = 4**

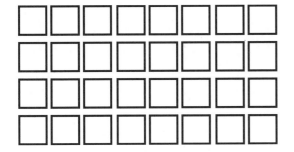

Think: 4 x _____ = 32

So, 32 ÷ _____ = 4.

4 **35 ÷ ? = 5**

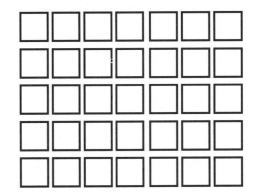

Think: 5 x _____ = 35

So, 35 ÷ _____ = 5.

⭐ **Tell how you can use multiplication to solve a division problem.**

Assessment

Complete each number sentence.

5 x _____ = 40

 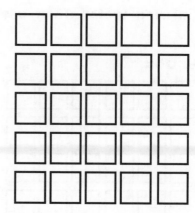

_____ = 25 ÷ 5

Circle the multiplication sentence that will help you find the quotient. Then write the quotient.

③ 12 ÷ 3 = _____

    2 x 3 = 6

    2 x 6 = 12

    3 x 4 = 12

④ 36 ÷ 4 = _____

    4 x 6 = 24

    4 x 9 = 36

    6 x 6 = 36

☆ **Tell** why you can use multiplication to solve each problem.

Overview   Understand Fractions

Directions and Sample Answers for Activity Pages

Day 1	See "Model the Skill" below.
Day 2	Read the directions aloud. Have students identify the total number of equal parts and then the number of parts that are shaded. (Answers: **1.** $\frac{1}{4}$; **2.** $\frac{1}{3}$; **3.** $\frac{1}{8}$; **4.** $\frac{1}{2}$)
Day 3	Read the directions aloud. Tell students that each shape is divided into equal parts. Help students see that the number of shaded parts is the numerator and the number of equal parts is the denominator. (Answers: **1.** 3; **2.** 6, 3; **3.** 5, $\frac{4}{5}$, 6; **4.** 2, 2) You might challenge students to identify the fraction that tells how many parts are NOT shaded.
Day 4	Read the directions aloud. Tell students that this time they will identify the fraction of the set that is shaded. Tell students that the numerator identifies the number of items that are shaded and the denominator names the total number of items in the set. (Answers: **1.** 1; **2.** 3; **3.** $\frac{2}{4}$; **4.** $\frac{5}{8}$)
Day 5	Read the directions aloud. Observe as students complete the page. Can they distinguish the numerator from the denominator? Do they understand that the shaded part is the numerator and the total number of parts is the denominator? Use your observations to plan further instruction and review. (Answers: **1.** 4; **2.** 2; **3.** 3, 5; **4.** 7, 8)

Model the Skill

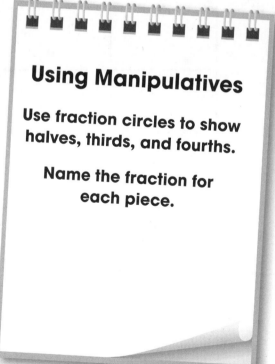

◆ Hand out the Day 1 activity page.

◆ **Say:** *Today we are going to learn about fractions. A fraction names part of a whole or part of a group. Look at problem 1. How many equal parts is the rectangle divided into? (2) Each part is one half of the whole rectangle.*

◆ Have students look at the fraction $\frac{1}{2}$ and point to the numerator. **Say:** *The numerator is the top number of a fraction. The numerator names a part of the whole.* Have students point to the denominator. **Say:** *The denominator is the bottom number of a fraction. The denominator tells how many equal parts are in the whole.*

Using Manipulatives

Use fraction circles to show halves, thirds, and fourths.

Name the fraction for each piece.

◆ Have students look at problem 2. **Ask:** *How many equal parts are in the whole? (3) What fraction names each part? ($\frac{1}{3}$)* Have students record the missing numerator.

◆ Help students complete the activity page and share their strategies for finding the missing numbers. They should recognize that the denominator is always the same as the number of equal parts. Have them identify whether the numerator or the denominator is the missing number in problems 3 and 4. (Answers: **3.** 4, 4; **4.** 8, 8)

Understand Fractions

Write each missing number.

3

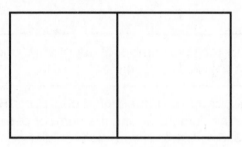

_____ equal parts

Each part is $\dfrac{1}{2}$.

2

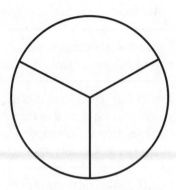

_____ equal parts

Each part is $\dfrac{\square}{3}$.

3

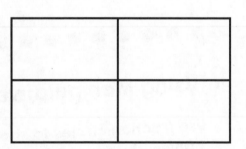

_____ equal parts

Each part is $\dfrac{1}{\square}$.

4

_____ equal parts

Each part is $\dfrac{1}{\square}$.

☆ **Tell how you found the missing numbers.**

Understand Fractions

Match the picture with the fraction that names the shaded part.

 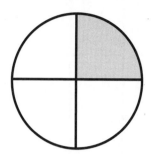 $\dfrac{1}{2}$

 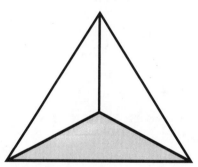 $\dfrac{1}{8}$

 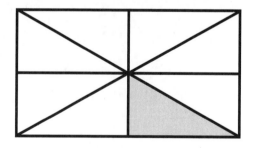 $\dfrac{1}{4}$

④ 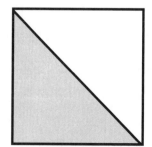 $\dfrac{1}{3}$

⭐ **Tell how you made each match.**

Understand Fractions

Write the missing numbers.

 ①
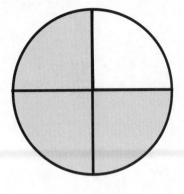

4 equal parts

$\dfrac{\square}{4}$ is shaded.

②
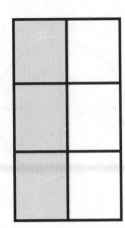

_____ equal parts

$\dfrac{\square}{6}$ is shaded.

③
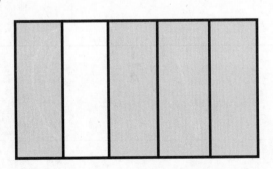

_____ equal parts

$\dfrac{\square}{\square}$ is shaded.

④
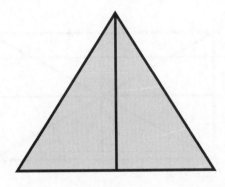

_____ equal parts

$\dfrac{\square}{2}$ is shaded.

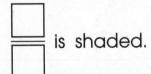 ☆ **Tell how you found the missing numbers.**

Understand Fractions

Name the shaded part. Complete each fraction.

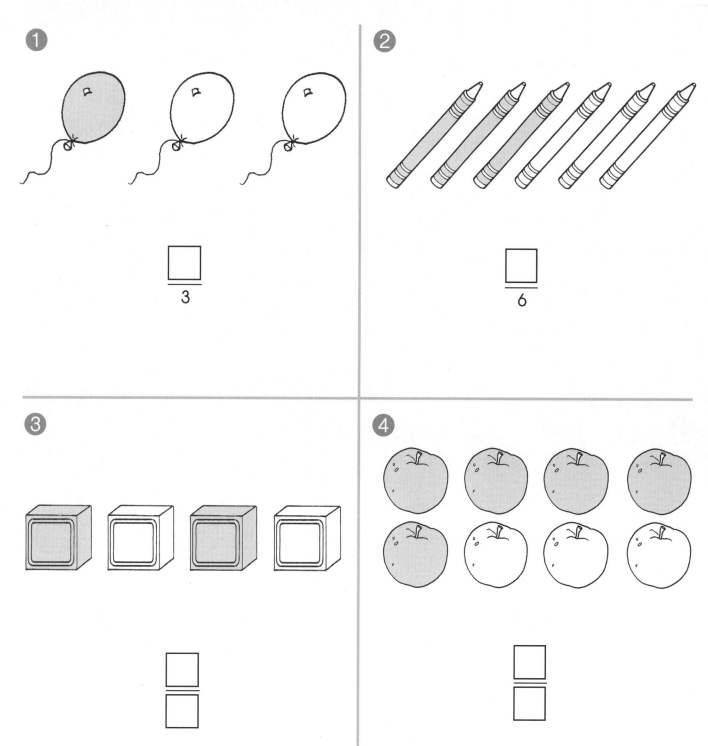

1

$$\frac{\boxed{}}{3}$$

2

$$\frac{\boxed{}}{6}$$

3

$$\frac{\boxed{}}{\boxed{}}$$

4

$$\frac{\boxed{}}{\boxed{}}$$

☆ **Tell how you know the fraction that matches each picture.**

Assessment

Write the fraction to name the shaded part.

1

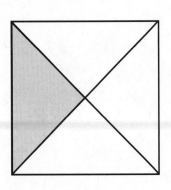

$$\frac{1}{\boxed{}}$$

2

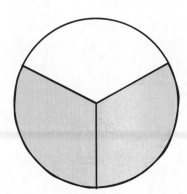

$$\frac{\boxed{}}{3}$$

3

$$\frac{\boxed{}}{\boxed{}}$$

4

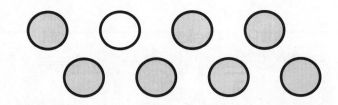

$$\frac{\boxed{}}{\boxed{}}$$

☆ **Tell how you know the numerator and denominator.**

Overview Fractions on a Number Line

Directions and Sample Answers for Activity Pages

Day 1	See "Model the Skill" below.
Day 2	Read the directions aloud. Have students identify the total number of equal parts and then draw a point to show the fraction. (Check students' work.)
Day 3	Read the directions aloud. Tell students that each number line is divided into equal parts, and that the number of equal parts is the denominator of each fraction. Have them identify the fraction above each tick mark. For problems 3 and 4, the point on the number line is not labeled. Remind them that the number line represents one whole. (Answers: **1.** $\frac{1}{4}$; **2.** $\frac{2}{3}$; **3.** $\frac{4}{6}$; **4.** $\frac{3}{8}$)
Day 4	Read the directions aloud. Tell students that for problems 1 and 2 they need to record only the numerator. Help them connect the denominators to the number of equal parts. (Answers: **1.** 3; **2.** 1; **3.** $\frac{2}{3}$; **4.** $\frac{6}{8}$)
Day 5	Read the directions aloud. Observe as students complete the page. Can they read the number line? Do they understand that the numerator is the number of parts from zero, and the denominator is the number of equal parts? (Answers: **1.** Check students' work. **2.** Check students' work. **3.** $\frac{2}{6}$ **4.** $\frac{2}{4}$)

Model the Skill

◆ Hand out the Day 1 activity page.

◆ **Say:** *You can use a number line to show fractions. Look at problem 1. How does the number line show equal parts?* (Possible response: The tick marks are spaced equally.) *How many equal spaces are there?* Help students count each equal part of the number line to verify that there are 3 equal parts.

◆ Point out the 0 and 1 under the first and last tick marks. **Say:** *The number line shows one whole. Each space is one equal part of the number line. Since this number line is divided into 3 equal spaces, we can say that it shows thirds.* Have students draw a line to show the match. (thirds)

◆ Have students look at problem 2. **Ask:** *How many equal parts does this number line have? Which word tells how this number line is divided?* (sixths)

◆ Help students complete the activity page and share their strategies for determining how to match the number line to how it is divided. (Answers: **3.** fourths; **4.** eighths)

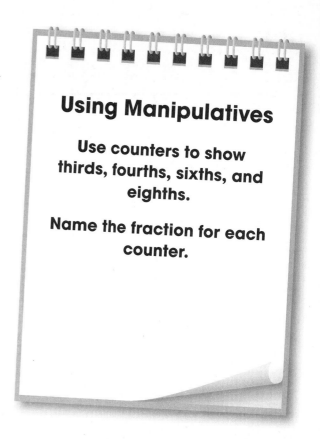

Using Manipulatives

Use counters to show thirds, fourths, sixths, and eighths.

Name the fraction for each counter.

Fractions on a Number Line

Match each number line to the equal parts it shows.

1

fourths

2

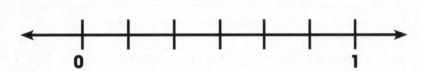

thirds

3

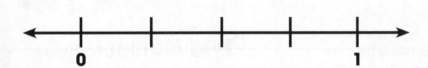

eighths

4

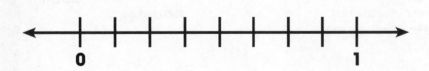

sixths

☆ **Tell how you know the number line matches the equal parts.**

Fractions on a Number Line

Draw a point on each number line to show the fraction.

 $\frac{1}{2}$

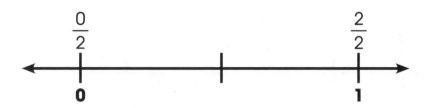

② $\frac{1}{8}$

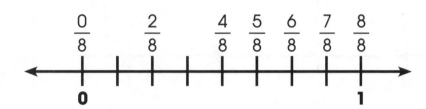

③ $\frac{1}{4}$

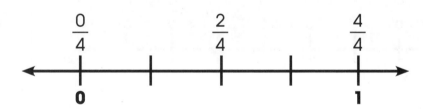

④ $\frac{1}{6}$

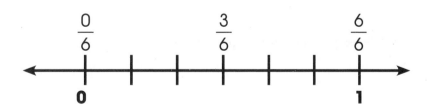

⭐ **Tell how you know the fraction matches the point on the number line.**

Fractions on a Number Line

Write a fraction that names each point.

1

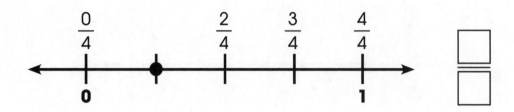

2

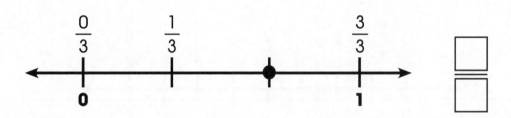

3

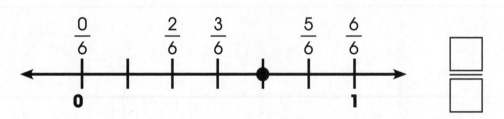

4

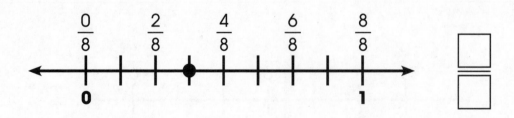

☆ **Tell how you found the fraction to name the point on the number line.**

Fractions on a Number Line

Write a fraction that names each point.

1

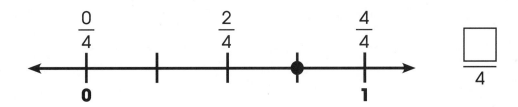

2

3

4

⭐ **Tell how you know what fraction to write.**

Assessment

Draw a point on each number line to show the fraction.

 $\frac{2}{4}$

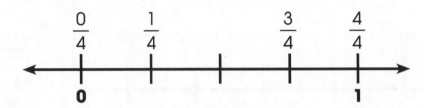

② $\frac{5}{8}$

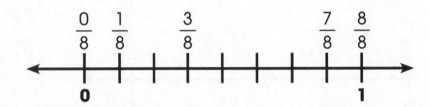

Write a fraction that names each point.

③

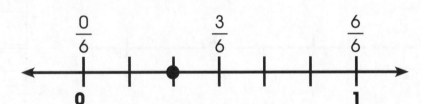

④

⭐ **Tell how you know the numerator and denominator.**

Overview Equivalent Fractions

Directions and Sample Answers for Activity Pages

Day 1	See "Model the Skill" below.
Day 2	Read the directions aloud. Tell students that they must record the numerator as well as the denominator for each problem. (Answers: **1.** $\frac{4}{6}$; **2.** $\frac{4}{4}$; **3.** $\frac{1}{2}$; **4.** $\frac{8}{8}$)
Day 3	Read the directions aloud. Tell students that for these problems they will be using a number line rather than fraction bars to find equivalent fractions. Help students identify the fractions shown on each number line. Help them to see that the same point on the number line can represent two different (and equivalent) fractions. (Answers: **1.** 1; **2.** 4; **3.** 6; **4.** 8)
Day 4	Read the directions aloud. Tell students to record the numerator as well as the denominator. In problems 3 and 4, help students realize that $\frac{2}{2}$, $\frac{4}{4}$, $\frac{6}{6}$, and $\frac{3}{3}$ all represent 1 whole. (Answers: **1.** $\frac{2}{6}$; **2.** $\frac{2}{8}$; **3.** $\frac{4}{4}$; **4.** $\frac{3}{3}$)
Day 5	Read the directions aloud. Observe as students complete the page. Can they identify equivalent fractions as having the same size? Do they understand that equivalent fractions share the same point on the number line? Use your observations to plan further instruction and review. (Answers: **1.** $\frac{6}{8}$; **2.** $\frac{4}{10}$; **3.** $\frac{4}{8}$; **4.** $\frac{6}{6}$)

Model the Skill

◆ Hand out the Day 1 activity page and fraction bars.

◆ **Say:** *Today we are going to learn about equivalent fractions. Equivalent fractions are fractions that are equal—they name the same amount.* Have students use fraction bars to model one-half in problem 1. **Say:** *We want to see how many fourths it takes to equal one-half.* Have students use fraction bars to model the fourths.

◆ **Ask:** *How many fourths are equal to one-half? How do you know?* (2; it takes two-fourths to be the same size as one-half.) **Say:** *One-half and two-fourths are the same size. One-half and two-fourths are equivalent fractions.* You might suggest that students place the fourths on top of the half as another way to show they are equal.

◆ Help students complete the activity page and share their strategies for finding the missing numerator. (Answers: **2.** 2; **3.** 2; **4.** 4)

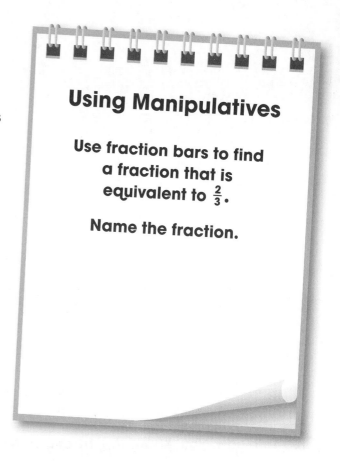

Using Manipulatives

Use fraction bars to find a fraction that is equivalent to $\frac{2}{3}$.

Name the fraction.

Name _____

Equivalent Fractions

Use fraction bars.
Write the missing numerator.

1

$\frac{1}{2}$

$\frac{1}{4}$	$\frac{1}{4}$

$$\frac{1}{2} = \frac{\square}{4}$$

2

$\frac{1}{4}$

$\frac{1}{8}$	$\frac{1}{8}$

$$\frac{1}{4} = \frac{\square}{8}$$

3

$\frac{1}{3}$

$\frac{1}{6}$	$\frac{1}{6}$

$$\frac{1}{3} = \frac{\square}{6}$$

4

$\frac{1}{4}$	$\frac{1}{4}$

$\frac{1}{8}$	$\frac{1}{8}$	$\frac{1}{8}$	$\frac{1}{8}$

$$\frac{2}{4} = \frac{\square}{8}$$

☆ **Tell how you know the fractions are equivalent.**

Equivalent Fractions

Use fraction bars.
Write an equivalent fraction to match the picture.

 1

$\dfrac{1}{3}$	$\dfrac{1}{3}$

$\dfrac{1}{6}$	$\dfrac{1}{6}$	$\dfrac{1}{6}$	$\dfrac{1}{6}$

$\dfrac{2}{3} \;=\; \dfrac{\square}{\square}$

2

$\dfrac{1}{3}$	$\dfrac{1}{3}$	$\dfrac{1}{3}$

$\dfrac{1}{4}$	$\dfrac{1}{4}$	$\dfrac{1}{4}$	$\dfrac{1}{4}$

$\dfrac{3}{3} \;=\; \dfrac{\square}{\square}$

3

$\dfrac{1}{2}$

$\dfrac{1}{10}$	$\dfrac{1}{10}$	$\dfrac{1}{10}$	$\dfrac{1}{10}$	$\dfrac{1}{10}$

$\dfrac{5}{10} \;=\; \dfrac{\square}{\square}$

4

$\dfrac{1}{4}$	$\dfrac{1}{4}$	$\dfrac{1}{4}$	$\dfrac{1}{4}$

$\dfrac{1}{8}$	$\dfrac{1}{8}$	$\dfrac{1}{8}$	$\dfrac{1}{8}$	$\dfrac{1}{8}$	$\dfrac{1}{8}$	$\dfrac{1}{8}$	$\dfrac{1}{8}$

$\dfrac{4}{4} \;=\; \dfrac{\square}{\square}$

⭐ **Tell how you know the fractions are equivalent.**

Equivalent Fractions

Use the number line.
Write the missing numerator or denominator.

1

$\dfrac{0}{4}$ $\dfrac{1}{4}$ $\dfrac{2}{4}$ $\dfrac{3}{4}$ $\dfrac{4}{4}$

$\dfrac{0}{2}$ $\dfrac{1}{2}$ $\dfrac{2}{2}$

$\dfrac{2}{4} \quad = \quad \dfrac{\boxed{}}{2}$

2

$\dfrac{0}{3}$ $\dfrac{1}{3}$ $\dfrac{2}{3}$ $\dfrac{3}{3}$

$\dfrac{0}{6}$ $\dfrac{1}{6}$ $\dfrac{2}{6}$ $\dfrac{3}{6}$ $\dfrac{4}{6}$ $\dfrac{5}{6}$ $\dfrac{6}{6}$

$\dfrac{2}{3} \quad = \quad \dfrac{\boxed{}}{6}$

3

$\dfrac{0}{4}$ $\dfrac{1}{4}$ $\dfrac{2}{4}$ $\dfrac{3}{4}$ $\dfrac{4}{4}$

$\dfrac{0}{8}$ $\dfrac{1}{8}$ $\dfrac{2}{8}$ $\dfrac{3}{8}$ $\dfrac{4}{8}$ $\dfrac{5}{8}$ $\dfrac{6}{8}$ $\dfrac{7}{8}$ $\dfrac{8}{8}$

$\dfrac{3}{4} \quad = \quad \dfrac{\boxed{}}{8}$

4

$\dfrac{0}{2}$ $\dfrac{1}{2}$ $\dfrac{2}{2}$

$\dfrac{0}{8}$ $\dfrac{4}{8}$ $\dfrac{8}{8}$

$\dfrac{1}{2} \quad = \quad \dfrac{4}{\boxed{}}$

☆ **Tell how you know the fractions are equivalent.**

Equivalent Fractions

Use the number line to write an equivalent fraction.

①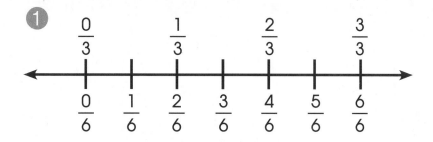

$$\frac{1}{3} = \frac{\Box}{\Box}$$

②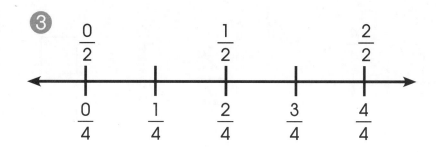

$$\frac{1}{4} = \frac{\Box}{\Box}$$

③

$$\frac{2}{2} = \frac{\Box}{\Box}$$

④

$$\frac{6}{6} = \frac{\Box}{\Box}$$

☆ **Tell how you know that 5/5 is also equivalent to 6/6.**

Name _____

Assessment

Use the fraction bars and number lines to write equivalent fractions.

1

$\frac{1}{4}$	$\frac{1}{4}$	$\frac{1}{4}$

$\frac{1}{8}$	$\frac{1}{8}$	$\frac{1}{8}$	$\frac{1}{8}$	$\frac{1}{8}$	$\frac{1}{8}$

$$\frac{3}{4} = \frac{\boxed{}}{\boxed{}}$$

2

$\frac{1}{5}$	$\frac{1}{5}$

$\frac{1}{10}$	$\frac{1}{10}$	$\frac{1}{10}$	$\frac{1}{10}$

$$\frac{2}{5} = \frac{\boxed{}}{\boxed{}}$$

3

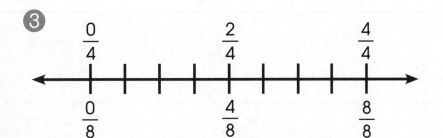

$$\frac{2}{4} = \frac{\boxed{}}{\boxed{}}$$

4

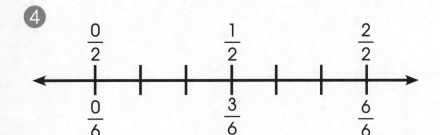

$$\frac{2}{2} = \frac{\boxed{}}{\boxed{}}$$

☆ **Tell a fraction that is equivalent to 2/2 and 6/6.**

Overview   Compare Fractions

Directions and Sample Answers for Activity Pages

Day 1	See "Model the Skill" below.
Day 2	Read the directions aloud. Tell students that they must record the symbol that makes each comparison true. Help students see that when the numerators are the same, the fraction with the lesser denominator is the greater fraction. (Answers: **1.** >; **2.** <; **3.** =; **4.** >)
Day 3	Read the directions aloud. Tell students that for these problems they will need to write the missing numerator or denominator that will make the comparison true. Point out that sometimes there may be more than one correct answer. (Answers may vary for problems 1, 3, and 4. **1.** Possible answer: 1; **2.** 2; **3.** Possible answer: 7; **4.** Possible answer: 3)
Day 4	Read the directions aloud. Allow students to use fraction models if they wish. Point out that sometimes there may be more than one correct answer. (Answers may vary for problems 1, 2, and 4. **1.** Possible answer: $\frac{1}{3}$; **2.** Possible answer: $\frac{1}{2}$; **3.** 1; **4.** Possible answer: $\frac{1}{4}$)
Day 5	Read the directions aloud. Allow students to use models if they wish. Observe as students complete the page. Do they record the comparison with the correct symbols? Do they compare fractions by reasoning about their size? Use your observations to plan further instruction and review. (Answers: **1.** <; **2.** <; **3.** >; **4.** =)

Model the Skill

◆ Hand out the Day 1 activity page and fraction bars.

◆ Remind students how they can use symbols to compare whole numbers. Review the meaning of the symbols: <, >, and =. **Say:** *Today we are going to use symbols to compare fractions.* Have students use fraction bars to model problem 1. **Say:** *When the denominators are the same, the fraction with the greater numerator is the greater fraction.* **Ask:** *Which is greater, $\frac{1}{3}$ or $\frac{2}{3}$?* ($\frac{2}{3}$) *How do you know?* (Possible response: When you look at the models, $\frac{2}{3}$ is larger than $\frac{1}{3}$.) **Say:** *$\frac{2}{3}$ is greater than $\frac{1}{3}$. Another way to say this is $\frac{1}{3}$ is less than $\frac{2}{3}$.* **Ask:** *What symbol will you write in the circle?* ("is less than" symbol) **Say:** *$\frac{1}{3}$ is less than $\frac{2}{3}$.*

◆ Help students complete the page. (Answers: **2.** >; **3.** <, **4.** =) Point out that when fractions in a pair have the same numerator and denominator, they are equal. **Say:** *$\frac{6}{6}$ is equal to $\frac{3}{3}$.*

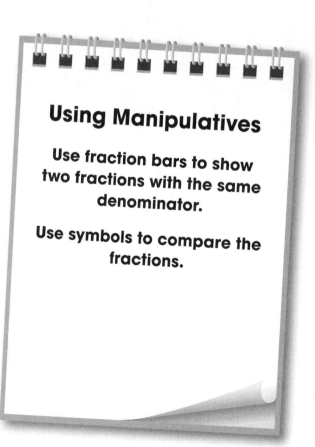

Using Manipulatives

Use fraction bars to show two fractions with the same denominator.

Use symbols to compare the fractions.

Name _____

Compare Fractions

Use fraction bars.

Compare the fractions. Write <, >, or =.

1 $\dfrac{1}{3}$ ◯ $\dfrac{2}{3}$

$\dfrac{1}{3}$

$\dfrac{1}{3}$	$\dfrac{1}{3}$

2 $\dfrac{4}{6}$ ◯ $\dfrac{3}{6}$

$\dfrac{1}{6}$	$\dfrac{1}{6}$	$\dfrac{1}{6}$	$\dfrac{1}{6}$

$\dfrac{1}{6}$	$\dfrac{1}{6}$	$\dfrac{1}{6}$

3 $\dfrac{2}{8}$ ◯ $\dfrac{5}{8}$

$\dfrac{1}{8}$	$\dfrac{1}{8}$

$\dfrac{1}{8}$	$\dfrac{1}{8}$	$\dfrac{1}{8}$	$\dfrac{1}{8}$	$\dfrac{1}{8}$

4 $\dfrac{6}{6}$ ◯ $\dfrac{3}{3}$

$\dfrac{1}{6}$	$\dfrac{1}{6}$	$\dfrac{1}{6}$	$\dfrac{1}{6}$	$\dfrac{1}{6}$	$\dfrac{1}{6}$

$\dfrac{1}{3}$	$\dfrac{1}{3}$	$\dfrac{1}{3}$

☆ **Tell how the fractions compare.**

 Unit 16 • Mathematics Intervention Activities Grade 3 • © 2014 Newmark Learning, LLC

Compare Fractions

Use fraction bars.

Compare the fractions. Write <, >, or =.

1 $\dfrac{1}{2}$ ◯ $\dfrac{1}{4}$

$\dfrac{1}{2}$

$\dfrac{1}{4}$

2 $\dfrac{1}{6}$ ◯ $\dfrac{1}{3}$

$\dfrac{1}{6}$

$\dfrac{1}{3}$

3 $\dfrac{3}{4}$ ◯ $\dfrac{3}{4}$

$\dfrac{1}{4}$	$\dfrac{1}{4}$	$\dfrac{1}{4}$

$\dfrac{1}{4}$	$\dfrac{1}{4}$	$\dfrac{1}{4}$

4 $\dfrac{2}{5}$ ◯ $\dfrac{2}{6}$

$\dfrac{1}{5}$	$\dfrac{1}{5}$

$\dfrac{1}{6}$	$\dfrac{1}{6}$

☆ **Tell which fraction is greater. Tell which fraction is lesser.**

Compare Fractions

Write a number to make each comparison true.

1

$$\frac{3}{4} > \frac{\square}{4}$$

2

$$\frac{2}{2} = \frac{2}{\square}$$

3

$$\frac{1}{8} < \frac{\square}{8}$$

4

$$\frac{4}{5} > \frac{\square}{5}$$

☆ **Tell which fraction is greater. Tell which fraction is lesser.**

Compare Fractions

Write a number to make each comparison true.

1

$$\frac{1}{2} > \frac{\boxed{}}{\boxed{}}$$

2

$$\frac{1}{8} < \frac{\boxed{}}{\boxed{}}$$

3

$$\frac{1}{6} = \frac{\boxed{}}{6}$$

4

$$\frac{1}{3} > \frac{\boxed{}}{\boxed{}}$$

☆ **Tell another way to compare the fractions.**

Assessment

Compare the fractions. Write <, >, or =.

 1

$$\frac{1}{8} \bigcirc \frac{1}{2}$$

 2

$$\frac{2}{8} \bigcirc \frac{5}{8}$$

3

$$\frac{3}{4} \bigcirc \frac{3}{6}$$

4

$$\frac{4}{4} \bigcirc \frac{3}{3}$$

☆ **Tell how you know each comparison is true.**

Overview   Time to the Minute

Directions and Sample Answers for Activity Pages

Day 1	See "Model the Skill" below.
Day 2	Read the directions aloud. Tell students that they must record the time by writing the hour before the colon and the minutes after the colon. Remind them to count the marks on the clock to determine the number of minutes before or after the hour. (Answers: **1.** 7:03, 3; **2.** 9:28, 28, 9; **3.** 11:47, 12; **4.** 1:56, 4, 2)
Day 3	Read the directions aloud. Tell students that for these problems they will need to first write the time shown on the clock, then write the time that the clock would show 10 minutes later. Allow students to use clock models if they wish. Encourage students to look for patterns. (Answers: **1.** 2:05, 2:15; **2.** 9:42, 9:52; **3.** 1:11, 1:21; **4.** 3:52, 4:02)
Day 4	Read the directions aloud. Some students may find it helpful to draw clock hands for the end time and then count the minute marks to determine the elapsed time. Some students may subtract to determine elapsed time. Have students share their strategies. (Answers: **1.** 22; **2.** 15; **3.** 16; **4.** 9)
Day 5	Read the directions aloud. Allow students to use clock models if they wish. Observe as students complete the page. Do they record the time in correct format? What strategies do they use to determine elapsed time? Use your observations to plan further instruction and review. (Answers: **1.** 5:12, 12, 5; **2.** 12:51, 9, 1; **3.** 20; **4.** 12)

Model the Skill

◆ Hand out the Day 1 activity page.

◆ Display a demonstration analog clock. Review the parts of the clock. Have students identify the hour hand, the minute hand, and the numbers on the clock face.

◆ **Ask:** *How can we use a clock to tell time?* (Possible response: look at the numbers that the hour hand and minute hand point to) **Say:** *The hour hand tells what hour it is. The minute hand tells how many minutes before or after the hour it is. There are 60 minutes in an hour. Each mark on the clock shows one minute. The marks on the clock can help us tell time to the minute.*

◆ Have students look at problem 1. **Ask:** *What number does the hour hand point to?* (3) *What number does the minute hand point to?* (20) *What time does the clock show?* (3:20; 3) Demonstrate how to record the time. Tell students that the colon separates the hours from the minutes.

◆ Help students complete the page. (Answers: **2.** 10:24, 24; **3.** 8:39, 39; **4.** 6:30, 6)

Using Manipulatives

Show a time on a clock.

Tell the time in different ways.

Name _____

Time to the Minute

Write the time two ways. Write the missing numbers.

1

_____ : _____

20 minutes after _____

2

_____ : _____

_____ minutes after 10

3

_____ : _____

_____ minutes after 8

4

_____ : _____

half past _____

☆ **Tell another way to tell the time.**

Time to the Minute

Write the time two ways. Write the missing numbers.

1

_____ : _____

_____ minutes after 7

2

_____ : _____

_____ minutes after _____

3

_____ : _____

13 minutes before _____

4

_____ : _____

_____ minutes before _____

☆ **Tell where the hour hand is pointing. Tell where the minute hand is pointing.**

Name _____

Time to the Minute

Write the time. Then write the time **10 minutes later.**

1

_____:_____

_____:_____

10 minutes later

2

_____:_____

_____:_____

10 minutes later

3

_____:_____

_____:_____

10 minutes later

4

_____:_____

_____:_____

10 minutes later

☆ **Tell where the clock hands point when it is 10 minutes later.**

 Unit 17 • Mathematics Intervention Activities Grade 3 • © 2014 Newmark Learning, LLC

Time to the Minute

Write how many minutes have passed.

Start at 4:00 A.M.

End at 4:22 A.M.

_____ minutes have passed.

Start at 8:30 A.M.

End at 8:45 A.M.

_____ minutes have passed.

Start at 10:40 P.M.

End at 10:56 P.M.

_____ minutes have passed.

Start at 2:58 A.M.

End at 3:07 A.M.

_____ minutes have passed.

 Tell how you know how many minutes have passed.

Assessment

Write the time two ways. Write the missing numbers.

1

_____:_____

_____ minutes after _____

2

_____:_____

_____ minutes before _____

Write how many minutes have passed.

3

Start at 7:35 P.M.

End at 7:55 P.M.

_____ minutes have passed.

4

Start at 4:18 P.M.

End at 4:30 A.M.

_____ minutes have passed.

☆ **Tell how you know how many minutes have passed.**

Overview Grams, Kilograms, Liters

Directions and Sample Answers for Activity Pages

Day 1	See "Model the Skill" below.
Day 2	Read the directions aloud. Observe if students understand the relationship of grams to kilograms. (Answers: **1.** 1 kilogram; **2.** 1 gram; **3.** 10 kilograms; **4.** 200 kilograms)
Day 3	Read the directions aloud. Using a liter bottle filled with water, help students check their estimates by pouring water from the liter into the container. Help students see that if there is still water in the liter bottle after filling the container, then the container holds less than a liter; if the liter bottle is empty and the container is not full, then the container holds more than a liter. Have students suggest a container for the bottom row of the chart.
Day 4	Read the directions aloud. Help students apply understanding of capacity and number sense to solve problems 1–4. (Answers: **1.** less than a liter; **2.** 1 liter; **3.** 50 liters; **4.** 3 liters)
Day 5	Read the directions aloud. Observe as students complete the page. Are students able to visualize standard units of grams, kilograms, and liters? Are they able to relate understanding of metric units of mass and capacity to real-life objects? Use your observations to plan further instruction and review. (Answers: **1.** 20 kilograms; **2.** 5 grams; **3.** 2 liters; **4.** 60 liters)

Model the Skill

◆ Hand out the Day 1 activity page. Have a balance and metric scale available.

◆ **Say:** *Today we are going to learn about mass. The mass of an object tells how heavy an object is. You can measure mass in grams or kilograms. One kilogram is equal in mass to 1,000 grams.* Display a balance and some gram weights. **Say:** *I could use grams and a balance to measure the mass of a crayon or an eraser. What other objects might I measure this way?* (Possible response: small, light objects such as paper or a pen) Allow students to brainstorm other objects that might be measured using grams and a balance, and other objects that might be measured using kilograms and a scale.

◆ Have students look at problem 1. Work together to estimate and then measure each of the objects in the chart. To help students estimate, have them hold the weights and the objects they will measure. Remind students that an estimate is a thoughtful guess.

◆ Help students complete problem 2 in a similar manner. **Ask:** *Would it be better to use grams or kilograms to measure the mass of a cat? Why?* (Possible response: kilograms because grams are too light) Have students suggest other items that might be measured in kilograms.

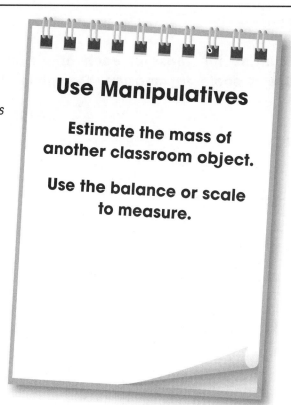

Use Manipulatives

Estimate the mass of another classroom object.

Use the balance or scale to measure.

Name _____

Grams, Kilograms, Liters

Estimate the mass of each object in grams.
Use a balance to measure. Complete the chart.

1 Mass of Small Objects

Object	Estimate	Measure
Pencil		
Paper cup		

Estimate the mass of each object in kilograms.
Use a scale to measure. Complete the chart.

2 Mass of Larger Objects

Object	Estimate	Measure
Stack of books		
Large bottle of water		

☆ **Name something that has a mass of about 1 kilogram.**

Unit 18 • Mathematics Intervention Activities Grade 3 • © 2014 Newmark Learning, LLC

Grams, Kilograms, Liters

Circle the better estimate of the mass of each item pictured.

bananas

1 gram

1 kilogram

paper clip

1 gram

1 kilogram

dog

10 grams

10 kilograms

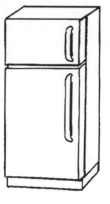

refrigerator

200 grams

200 kilograms

 Tell how you know your answer is reasonable.

Grams, Kilograms, Liters

Estimate the capacity of each container in liters. Is it more or less than a liter?
Write *more* or *less*. Then use a liter to measure.

Capacity

Object	Estimate More or less than a liter?	Measure More or less than a liter?
Paper cup		
Large bottle		
Teaspoon		
Write your own.		

⭐ **Tell something that has a capacity of about 1 liter.**

Unit 18 • Mathematics Intervention Activities Grade 3 • © 2014 Newmark Learning, LLC

Grams, Kilograms, Liters

How much will each container hold?
Circle the better estimate.

drinking glass

more than a liter

less than a liter

water bottle

1 liter

10 liters

 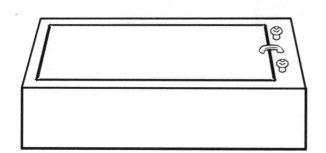

bathtub

5 liters

50 liters

saucepan

3 liters

30 liters

 Tell how you know your answers are reasonable.

Assessment

Circle the better estimate of the mass of each object.

①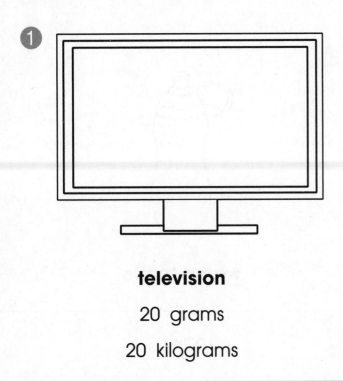

television

20 grams

20 kilograms

②

nickel

5 grams

5 kilograms

Circle the better estimate of the volume of each object.

③

pitcher

2 liters

20 liters

④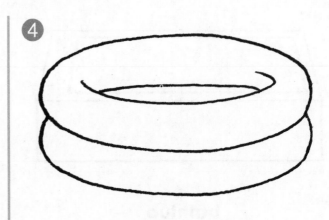

swimming pool

6 liters

60 liters

⭐ **Name something that has a capacity of less than a liter.**

Overview   Measure Length to the Nearest Quarter Inch

Directions and Sample Answers for Activity Pages

Day 1	See "Model the Skill" below.
Day 2	Read the directions aloud. Discuss how measuring to the nearest quarter inch is different from measuring to the nearest half inch. Help students see that the quarter-inch measurement is more exact. (Answers: **1.** $3\frac{1}{4}$; **2.** $4\frac{3}{4}$ **3.** 2)
Day 3	Read the directions aloud. Discuss how to read the tally marks. Tell students that the tally marks for crayons that are 3 inches long and $3\frac{1}{4}$ inches long have already been entered. Help students complete the line plot. (Check students' work.)
Day 4	Read the directions aloud. Provide students with inch rulers marked with halves and fourths. Provide crayons that are between 3 and 4 inches in length. Observe if students correctly align the crayons with the beginning of the ruler. Help them record and plot the data. (Check students' work.)
Day 5	Read the directions aloud. Provide students with inch rulers marked with halves and fourths. Observe as students complete the page. Do they understand how to measure to the nearest half inch? Do they plot the data correctly? Use your observations to plan further instruction and review. (Answers: **1.** 4; **2.** $3\frac{1}{2}$; **3.** 2; **4.** $3\frac{1}{2}$; **5.** 2; **6.** $2\frac{1}{2}$; **7.** $3\frac{1}{2}$)

Model the Skill

◆ Hand out the Day 1 activity page.

◆ **Say:** *You can use an inch ruler to measure the length of an object.* Have students look at the ruler in problem 1. Help them identify the $\frac{1}{4}$-inch and $\frac{1}{2}$-inch marks on the ruler. Point out that the $\frac{1}{2}$-inch mark is the same as $\frac{2}{4}$. Have students identify specific points on the ruler, such as $1\frac{1}{2}$ inches, $2\frac{1}{4}$ inches, and $4\frac{3}{4}$ inches.

Use Manipulatives

Use a ruler to find the length of your pencil to the nearest half inch.

◆ **Ask:** *What is the length of the pencil to the nearest inch?* (5 inches) *How did you find your answer?* (Possible response: I looked for the number on the ruler that is closest to the point of the pencil.) **Say:** *Look at the dashed lines at each end of the pencil. The first line shows you that the pencil and the ruler begin at the same place. The second line shows you how many inches long the pencil is.*

◆ **Say:** *Now let's find the length of the pencil to the nearest half inch. Between which two marks is the end of the pencil?* ($5\frac{1}{4}$ and $5\frac{1}{2}$) *Is the pencil closer to 5 inches or $5\frac{1}{2}$ inches?* ($5\frac{1}{2}$ inches) **Say:** *We can say the length of the ruler is $5\frac{1}{2}$ inches to the nearest half inch.*

◆ Help students complete problems 2–3 in a similar manner. Provide students with rulers marked with halves and fourths to use if they wish. Ask students to explain how they found their answers. (Answers: **2.** 4; **3.** $2\frac{1}{2}$)

Name _____

Measure Length to the Nearest Quarter Inch

Measure the length of each pencil to the nearest half inch.

① _____ inches

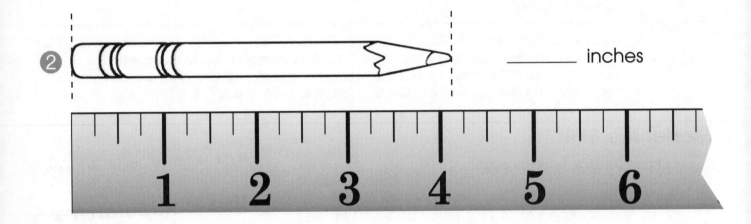

② _____ inches

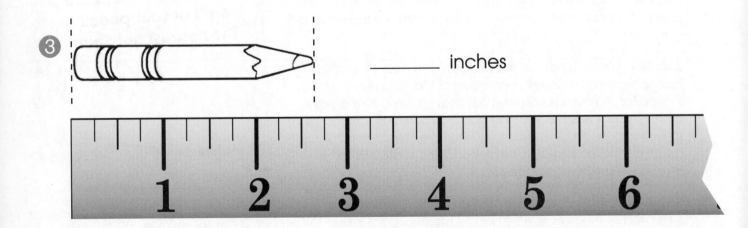

③ _____ inches

☆ **Tell how you measured.**

Measure Length to the Nearest Quarter Inch

Measure the length of each string to the nearest quarter inch.

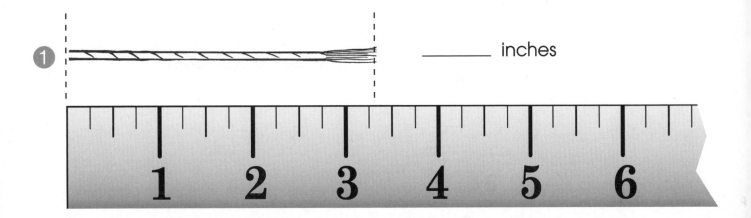

1 _____ inches

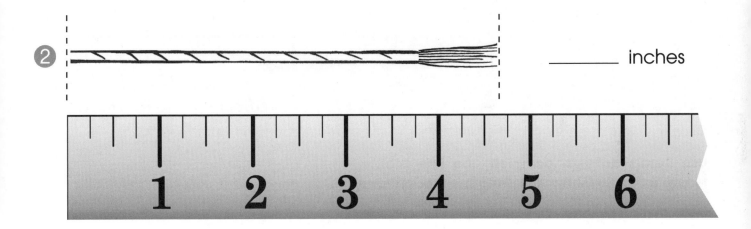

2 _____ inches

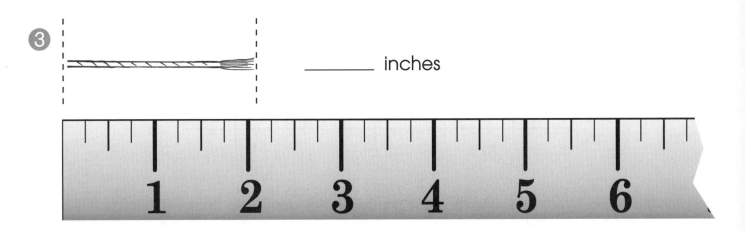

3 _____ inches

☆ **Tell how you measured.**

Measure Length to the Nearest Quarter Inch

Sam measured the lengths of his crayons.

The table shows his data.

Length of Crayons in Inches	Number of Crayons
3	|
$3\frac{1}{4}$	|||
$3\frac{1}{2}$	~~||||~~
$3\frac{3}{4}$	|
4	

Use Sam's data to complete the line plot.
Make an X to show the length of each crayon.

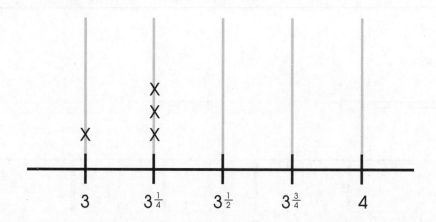

Length of Crayons in Inches

⭐ **Tell what the line plot shows.**

Name _____

Measure Length to the Nearest Quarter Inch

Use an inch ruler.
Measure the length of 10 crayons.
Measure to the nearest quarter inch.
Record the data.

Length of Crayons in Inches	Number of Crayons
3	
$3\frac{1}{4}$	
$3\frac{1}{2}$	
$3\frac{3}{4}$	
4	

Use the data to make a line plot.
Make an X to show the length of each crayon.

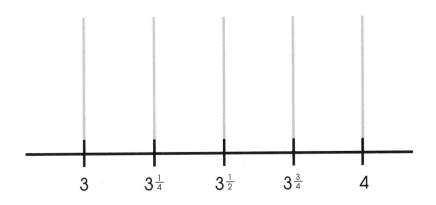

Length of Crayons in Inches

☆ **Tell how the data in the chart matches the line plot.**

Assessment

Use an inch ruler.

Measure each string to the nearest half inch.

① 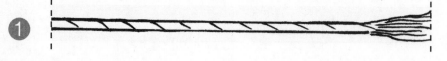 _____ inches

② 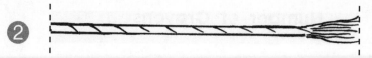 _____ inches

③  _____ inches

④ 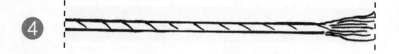 _____ inches

⑤ 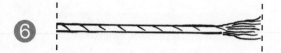 _____ inches

⑥ 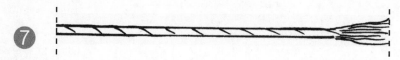 _____ inches

⑦ 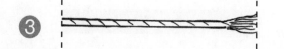 _____ inches

Use the data to make a line plot.

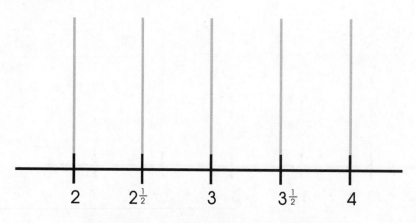

Length of String in Inches

☆ **Tell which length you found most.**

Overview Make and Use Pictographs and Bar Graphs

Directions and Sample Answers for Activity Pages

Day 1	See "Model the Skill" below.
Day 2	Read the directions aloud. Point out that there is already 1 ticket drawn in the first row. Tell students that each rectangle they draw will stand for 4 tickets. Ask how they could represent 2 tickets. Discuss strategies for answering "how many more" and "how many fewer" questions. (Answers: **1.** Check students' work; **2.** 2; **3.** 8; **4.** 6)
Day 3	Read the directions aloud. Discuss how a bar graph is different from a pictograph. Help students identify the number of votes for each animal. (Answers: **1.** 4; **2.** 2; **3.** 3; **4.** 7)
Day 4	Read the directions aloud. Tell students that the graph is a vertical bar graph and that the space between two horizontal lines represents 4 books. Ask how they could represent 2 books. (Answers: **1.** Check students' work; **2.** 4; **3.** 8; **4.** 2)
Day 5	Read the directions aloud. Observe as students complete the page. Do they understand how to answer "how many more" and "how many fewer" questions? Do they know how to complete a bar graph? Use your observations to plan further instruction and review. (Answers: **1.** 8; **2.** 6; **3.** 4; **4.** check students' work.)

Model the Skill

◆ Hand out the Day 1 activity page.

◆ **Say:** *Today we are going to learn about pictographs. Pictographs are graphs that use pictures or symbols to show information or data.* Have students look at the pictograph on the page. **Ask:** *What is the title of the graph?* (Favorite Juices) *What are the juice choices?* (apple, pineapple, grape, and orange) *What does each cup stand for?* (2 votes) *How do you know?* (Possible response: the sentence under the graph tells you.) You may wish to point out that the sentence under the graph is called the "key."

◆ Have students look at question 1. **Ask:** *Which juice got the most votes? How do you know?* (apple; possible explanation: that row is the longest; it has the most cups.) Have students share their strategies.

◆ Help students answer question 2. **Ask:** *What information do we need to answer question 2?* (how many students voted for apple and how many voted for orange) *How can you tell by looking at the graph?* (Possible response: I see there is 1 more cup for apple than orange. That means 2 more students voted for apple.) Have students discuss other strategies such as subtracting the number of votes for orange juice from the number of votes for apple juice.

◆ Help students answer questions 3 and 4 and share their strategies. (Answers: **3.** 5; **4.** 6)

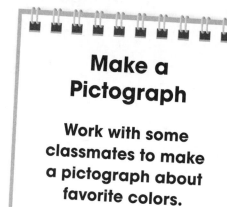

Make a Pictograph

Work with some classmates to make a pictograph about favorite colors.

Make and Use Pictographs and Bar Graphs

Mr. Smith's class made a pictograph.

The graph shows the students' favorite juice.

Use the pictograph to answer each question.

Favorite Juices

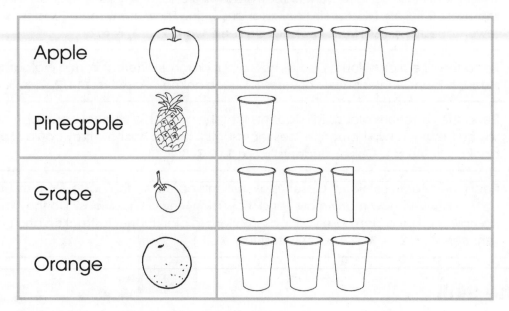

Each ⎍ **stands for 2 votes.**

① Which juice got the most votes? _____

② How many more students voted for apple juice than orange juice?
_____ more students

③ How many students voted for grape juice? _____ students

④ How many fewer students voted for pineapple juice than
apple juice? _____ fewer students

⭐ **Tell how you got your answers.**

Make and Use Pictographs and Bar Graphs

Jan sold 12 tickets to the class play.

Pat sold 4 tickets.

Ben sold 6 tickets.

① **Complete the pictograph. Show how many tickets each child sold.**

Tickets Sold

Jan	ADMIT ONE
Pat	
Ben	

Each ADMIT ONE **stands for 4 tickets.**

Use the graph to answer each question.

② How many more tickets did Ben sell than Pat?

_____ more tickets

③ How many fewer tickets did Pat sell than Jan?

_____ fewer tickets

④ How many fewer tickets did Ben sell than Jan?

_____ fewer tickets

⭐ **Tell how the pictograph shows how many tickets Ben sold.**

Make and Use Pictographs and Bar Graphs

The students in Mr. Gold's class voted for their favorite farm animal.

The bar graph shows the results.

Use the bar graph to answer each question.

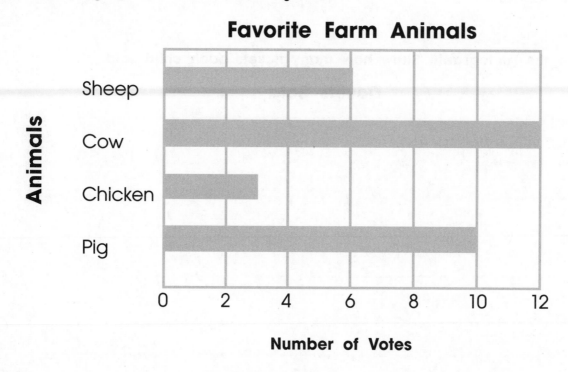

Favorite Farm Animals

1️⃣ How many more students voted for pig than sheep?

_____ more students

2️⃣ How many fewer students voted for pig than cow?

_____ fewer students

3️⃣ How many more students voted for sheep than chicken?

_____ students

4️⃣ How many fewer students voted for chicken than pig?

_____ fewer students

⭐ **Tell how you got your answers.**

Make and Use Pictographs and Bar Graphs

Gia read 12 books during the summer.

Sandy read 16 books. Jon read 10 books.

Tim read 8 books.

1 Complete the bar graph. Show how many books each student read.

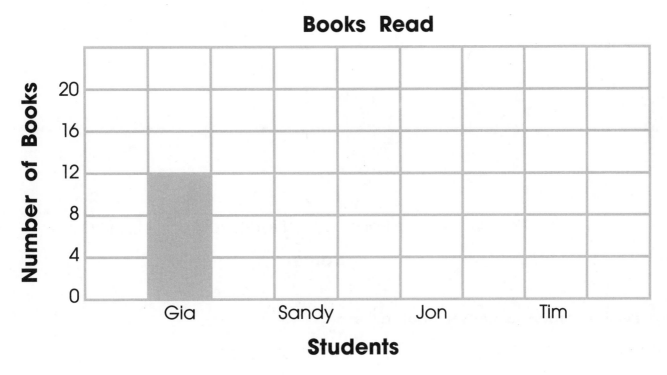

Books Read

Use the graph to answer each question.

2 How many more books did Sandy read than Gia?

_____ more books

3 How many fewer books did Tim read than Sandy?

_____ fewer books

4 How many more books did Jon read than Tim?

_____ more books

⭐ **Tell how the bar graph shows how many books Jon read.**

Assessment

The bar graph shows the number of items sold at the school store.

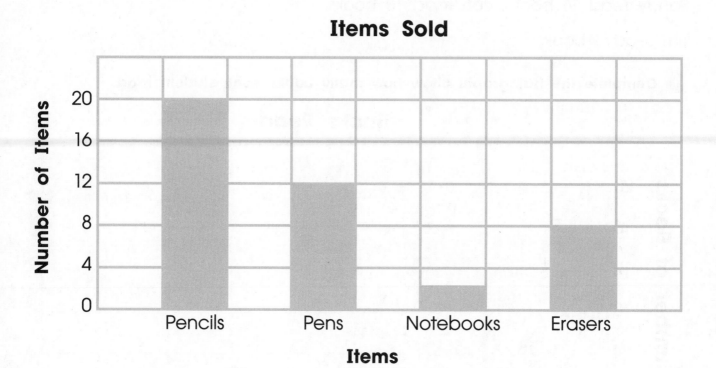

Use the bar graph to answer each question.

1 How many more pencils were sold than pens?

_____ more pencils

2 How many more erasers were sold than notebooks?

_____ more erasers

3 How many fewer erasers were sold than pens?

_____ fewer erasers

4 What if 4 notepads were also sold? Draw a bar on the graph
to show the notepads. Label the bar you draw.

☆ **Tell how you know the bar shows 4 notepads.**

Overview   Understand Perimeter

Directions and Sample Answers for Activity Pages

Day 1	See "Model the Skill" below.
Day 2	Read the directions aloud. Tell students that a closed figure has no open space—it begins and ends at the same point. Tell students that a rectangle and a triangle are examples of closed figures. (Check students' work.)
Day 3	Read the directions aloud. Remind students that the perimeter is the distance around a figure. Tell students that another way to find the perimeter of a figure is to add the number of units on each side. (Answers: **1.** 16, 16; **2.** 9, 9; **3.** 14, 14; **4.** 18, 18)
Day 4	Read the directions aloud. Have students identify the given lengths of each side of the figure and point to the side of the figure with the missing length. Discuss strategies for finding the missing length. (Answers: **1.** 2; **2.** 5; **3.** 3; **4.** 5)
Day 5	Read the directions aloud. Observe as students complete the page. Do they understand how to find the perimeter of a figure? Use your observations to plan further instruction and review. (Answers: **1.** 12; **2.** 20; **3.** 20)

Model the Skill

◆ Hand out the Day 1 activity page.

◆ **Say:** *Today we are going to learn about perimeter. Perimeter is the distance around a figure.* Have students look at problem 1. Demonstrate how to find the length of each side.

◆ **Ask:** *What shape is this figure?* (rectangle) *What is the perimeter? How do you know?* (12 units; possible explanation: there are 12 units around the rectangle, so the perimeter is 12; add the length of each side)

◆ Have students look at problem 2. **Ask:** *How is this figure different from the figure in problem 1?* (Possible response: this is not a rectangle; this figure looks like a square with an extra square unit.) Point out that students can still tell the perimeter of the figure by counting the number of units. Help students find the length of each side.

◆ Help students complete the activity page. (Answers: **2.** 10; **3.** 8; **4.** 12)

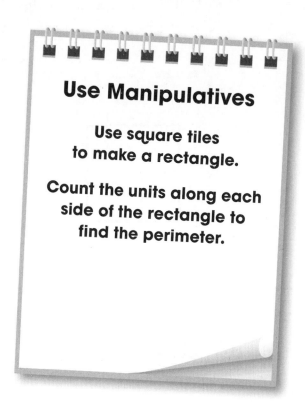

Use Manipulatives

Use square tiles to make a rectangle.

Count the units along each side of the rectangle to find the perimeter.

Understand Perimeter

Find the perimeter. Count the units.

1

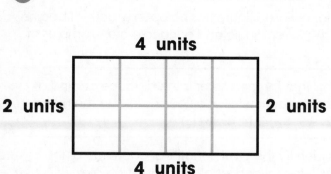

Perimeter: _____ units

2

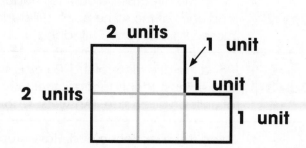

Perimeter: _____ units

3

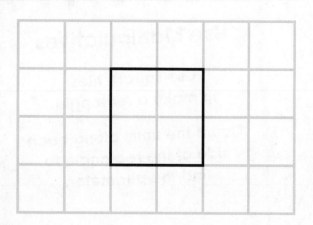

Perimeter: _____ units

4

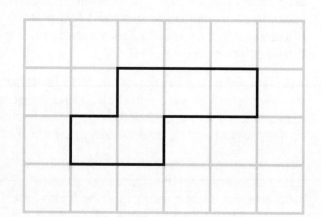

Perimeter: _____ units

☆ **Tell how you counted the units to find the perimeter.**

Understand Perimeter

Draw a closed figure. Write the perimeter.

1

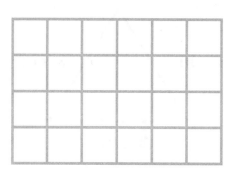

Perimeter: _____ units

2

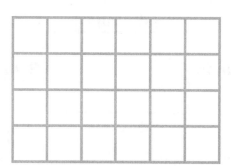

Perimeter: _____ units

Draw a closed figure to match the perimeter.

3

Perimeter: 8 units

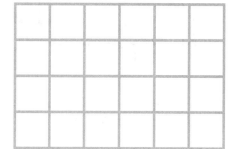

4

Perimeter: 10 units

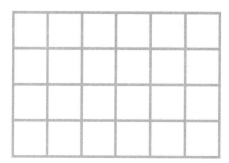

⭐ **Tell how you found the perimeter.**

Name _____

Understand Perimeter

Add to find the perimeter.

①

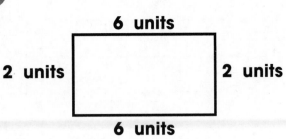

6 units

2 units   2 units

6 units

2 + 6 + 2 + 6 = _____

Perimeter: _____ units

②

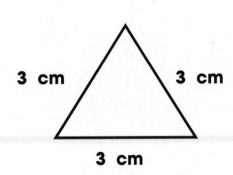

3 cm   3 cm

3 cm

3 + 3 + 3 = _____

Perimeter: _____ centimeters

③

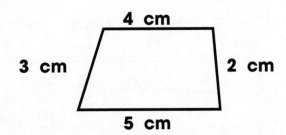

4 cm

3 cm   2 cm

5 cm

3 + 4 + 2 + 5 = _____

Perimeter: _____ centimeters

④

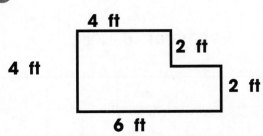

4 ft

2 ft

4 ft

2 ft

6 ft

4 + 4 + 2 + 2 + 6 = _____

Perimeter: _____ feet

☆ **Tell how you found the perimeter.**

Understand Perimeter

Find the missing length.

1

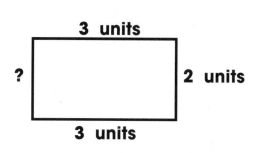

3 units

?   2 units

3 units

Perimeter: 10 units

Length of missing side:

_____ units

2

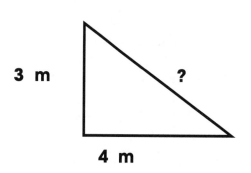

3 m   ?

4 m

Perimeter: 12 meters

Length of missing side:

_____ meters

3

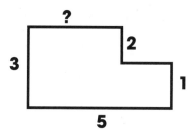

?

3   2

1

5

Perimeter: 14 units

Length of missing side:

_____ units

4

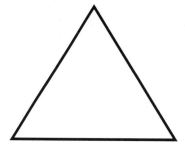

The perimeter of this triangle is 15 meters.

Each side has the same length.

What is the length of each side?

_____ meters

⭐ **Tell how you found your answer.**

Name _____

Assessment

Find the perimeter of each figure.

1

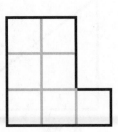

Perimeter: _____ units

2

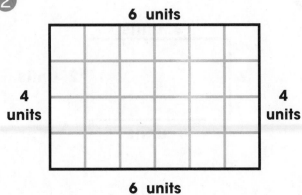

6 units

4 units   4 units

6 units

Perimeter: _____ units

3

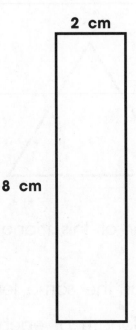

2 cm

8 cm

Perimeter: _____ centimeters

⭐ **Tell** how you found the perimeter.

Unit 21 • Mathematics Intervention Activities Grade 3 • © 2014 Newmark Learning, LLC

Overview Understand Area

Directions and Sample Answers for Activity Pages

Day 1	See "Model the Skill" below.
Day 2	Read the directions aloud. Tell students that they can draw any figure they like as long as the area is the given number of square units. Point out that there are many different figures that could have the same area. Have students find the perimeter of the figures. Discuss the difference between perimeter and area. (Check students' work.)
Day 3	Read the directions aloud. Have students identify each figure as a rectangle. Discuss how the addition sentences in problems 1 and 2 reflect the number of rows and columns in each figure. (Answers: **1.** 12, 12; **2.** 10, 10; **3.** Possible answer: 3 + 3 + 3 + 3 + 3 = 15, 15; **4.** Possible answer: 7 + 7 + 7 + 7 = 28)
Day 4	Read the directions aloud. Have students identify each figure as a rectangle. Help them connect the number of rows and columns in each rectangle to its length and width. (Answers: **1.** 6, 6; **2.** 8, 8; **3.** Possible answer: 4 x 3 = 12, 12; **4.** Possible answer: 3 x 5= 15, 15)
Day 5	Read the directions aloud. Observe as students complete the page. Do they understand that area can be measured in square units? Do they understand how to use addition or multiplication to find the area of a rectangle? Use your observations to plan further instruction and review. (Answers: **1.** 2 x 4 = 8 square units; **2.** 4 + 4 + 4 + 4 = 16 square units; **3.** 4 x 8 = 32 square units; **4.** 3 + 3 + 3 = 9 square units)

Model the Skill

◆ Hand out the Day 1 activity page.

◆ **Say:** *Today we are going to learn about area. Area is the number of square units that are needed to cover a flat surface.* Have students look at problem 1 and identify one square unit. **Ask:** *What figure do the square units make?* (rectangle) **Say:** *You can count the square units in the rectangle to find its area. How many square units are in the rectangle?* (6) *We can say that the area of this rectangle is 6 square units.* Tell students to write the area in the space provided.

◆ Have students look at problem 2. **Ask:** *How is this figure different from the figure in problem 1?* (Possible response: This is not a rectangle; this figure has many sides that go in and out.) Point out that students can still tell the area of the figure by counting the number of square units. (7) Allow students to use square tiles if they wish to model the figure, and then find the area.

◆ Help students complete the activity page. (Answers: **3.** 12; **4.** 10)

Use Manipulatives

Use square tiles to make a figure.

Count the tiles to find the area of the figure.

Name _____

Understand Area

Count the square units to find the area.

 1

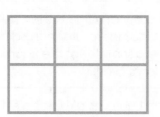

_____ square units

2

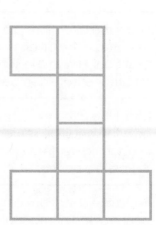

_____ square units

3

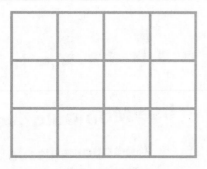

_____ square units

4

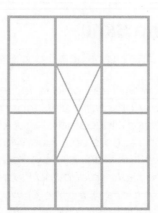

_____ square units

☆ **Tell how you got your answer.**

Understand Area

Draw a figure to match the area.

①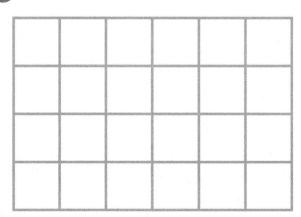

4 square units

②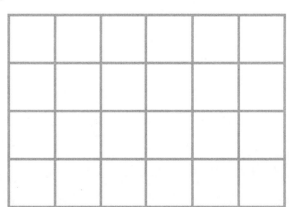

9 square units

③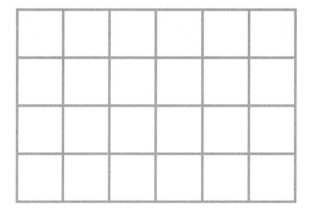

8 square units

④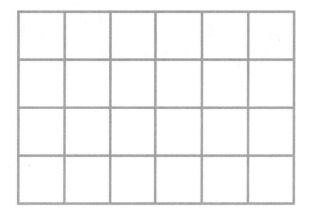

12 square units

☆ **Tell how you know your figure shows an area of 12 square units.**

Name _____

Understand Area

Add to find the area.

 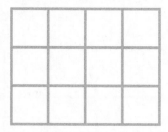

4 squares in each row, 3 rows

4 + 4 + 4 = _____

Area: _____ square units

②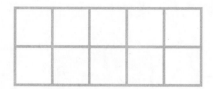

___ squares in each row, ___ rows

5 + 5 = _____

Area: _____ square units

Write an addition sentence to find the area.

③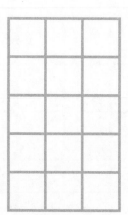

_____

Area: _____ square units

④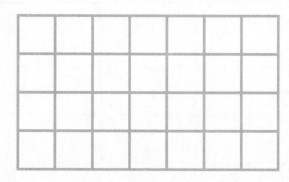

_____

Area: _____ square units

⭐ **Tell another addition sentence you can use to find the area.**

Understand Area

Multiply to find the area.

1

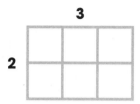

2 x 3 = _____

Area: _____ square units

2

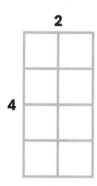

4 x 2 = _____

Area: _____ square units

Write a multiplication sentence to find the area.

3

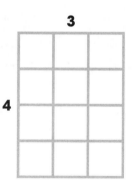

_____ x _____ = _____

Area: _____ square units

4

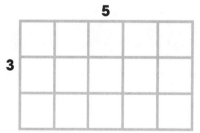

_____ x _____ = _____

Area: _____ square units

☆ **Tell another multiplication sentence you can use to find the area.**

Assessment

Match the rectangle to the number sentence you can use to find the area.
Then find the area.

1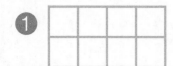

$$3 + 3 + 3 = \boxed{}$$

_____ square units

2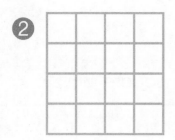

$$4 \times 8 = \boxed{}$$

_____ square units

3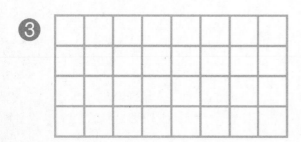

$$4 + 4 + 4 + 4 = \boxed{}$$

_____ square units

4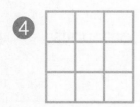

$$2 \times 4 = \boxed{}$$

_____ square units

☆ **Tell how you know the number sentence matches the figure.**

23

Overview Quadrilaterals

Directions and Sample Answers for Activity Pages

Day 1	See "Model the Skill" below.
Day 2	Read the directions aloud. Help students identify the shape of each figure. Remind them that rectangles and squares have four right angles. (Answers: The following figures in each row should be crossed out: **1.** first figure; **2.** second figure; **3.** first figure)
Day 3	Read the directions aloud. Tell students that there is more than one figure in each row that does not belong with the others. Invite students to share and justify their answers. (Answers: The following figures in each row should be crossed out: **1.** first, third, and fourth figures; **2.** first, second, and fifth figures; **3.** second, fourth, and fifth figures)
Day 4	Read the directions aloud. Allow students to use geoboards and rubber bands to create each figure before drawing it. Have students share their work and explain how their figures match the descriptions. (Check students' work.)
Day 5	Read the directions aloud. Do students understand that different shapes may share some of the same attributes? Do they recognize rhombuses, rectangles, and squares as examples of quadrilaterals? Use your observations to plan further instruction and review. (Answers: **1.** The first, fourth, and fifth figures should have rings; **2.** The third and fifth figures should have rings around them; **3.** The second, third, and fourth figures should be crossed out; **4.** Check students' work.)

Model the Skill

◆ Hand out the Day 1 activity page.

◆ **Say:** *We are going to learn about quadrilaterals today. A quadrilateral is a plane figure with 4 sides. A plane figure is a closed figure—it begins and ends at the same place.* Have students identify the open and closed figures in problem 1; then call their attention to the first figure in the row.

◆ **Ask:** *What shape is this figure?* (square) *How do you know the figure is a square?* (Possible response: It has 4 sides and 4 right angles.) *Is a square a quadrilateral? How do you know?* (Yes; it is a plane figure with 4 sides.) Have students draw a ring around the square.

◆ Have students look at the second figure. **Ask:** *What shape is this figure?* (open figure) *How many sides does this figure have? Is this figure a quadrilateral? Why or why not?* (No; It has 5 sides and it is not a closed figure.) Help students identify and draw rings around the remaining quadrilaterals in problem 1. (Answer: **1.** first, third, and fourth)

◆ **Say:** *Now look at problem 2. Is this figure a quadrilateral? Why or why not?* (No; it is not a plane figure; it is a rectangular prism.) Help students identify and draw rings around the remaining quadrilaterals in problems 2–4. (Answers: The following figures in each row should have rings: **2.** second, fourth, and fifth; **3.** first, fourth, and fifth; **4.** fourth and fifth)

Use Manipulatives

Use a geoboard and rubber bands.

Make figures that are quadrilaterals.

Quadrilaterals

Draw a ring around each quadrilateral.

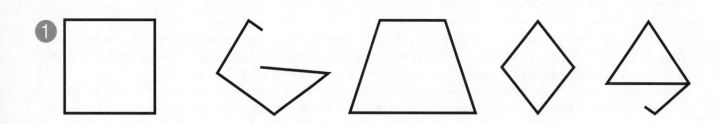

1

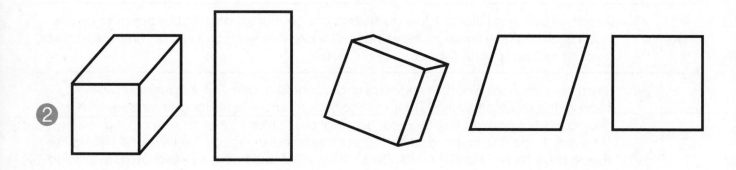

2

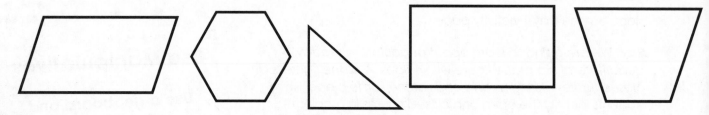

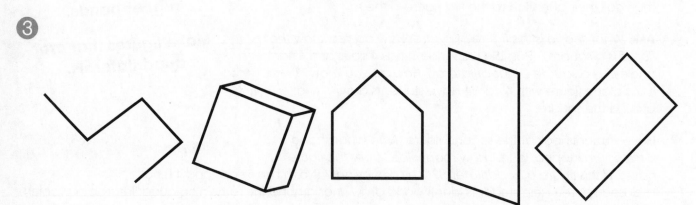

3

☆ **Tell how you know which figure is a quadrilateral.**

Unit 23 • Mathematics Intervention Activities Grade 3 • © 2014 Newmark Learning, LLC

Quadrilaterals

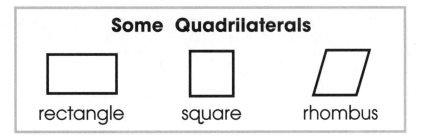

Cross out the figure that does NOT belong.

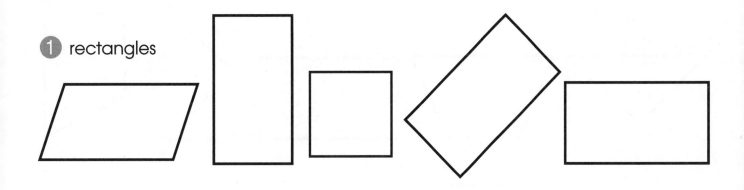

1 rectangles

2 squares

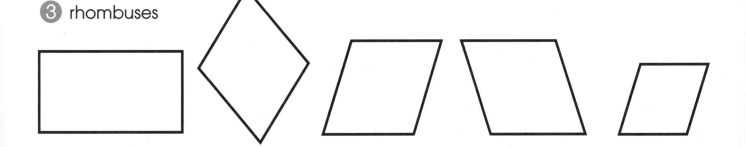

3 rhombuses

⭐ **Tell how a rhombus and a square are different.**

Quadrilaterals

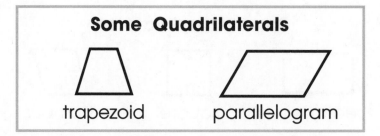

Some Quadrilaterals

trapezoid   parallelogram

Cross out the figures that do NOT belong.

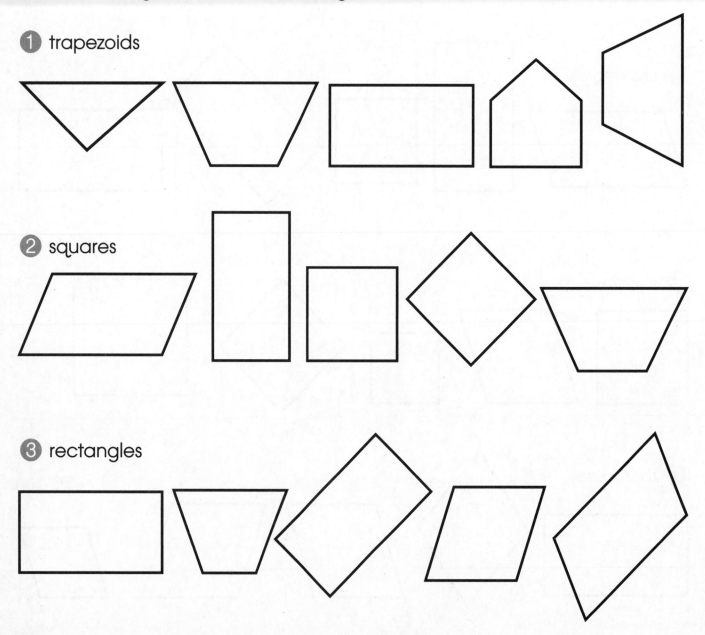

1 trapezoids

2 squares

3 rectangles

⭐ **Tell how a rectangle and a trapezoid are different.**

Quadrilaterals

Draw each figure.

1 quadrilateral with 4 sides of equal lengths

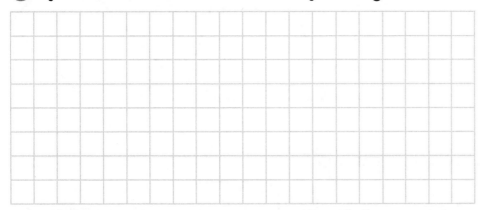

2 quadrilateral that is NOT a rectangle

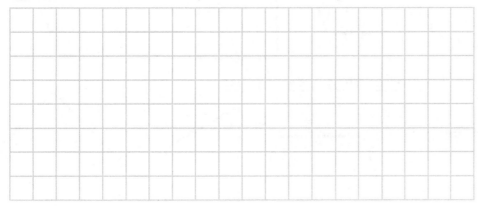

3 quadrilateral that does NOT have 4 right angles

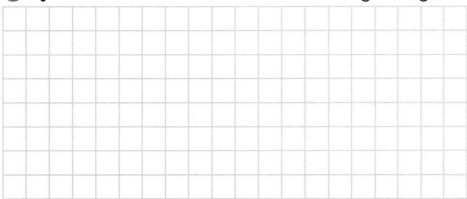

☆ **Tell what makes your drawing a quadrilateral.**

Name _____

Assessment

1 Draw a ring around each quadrilateral.

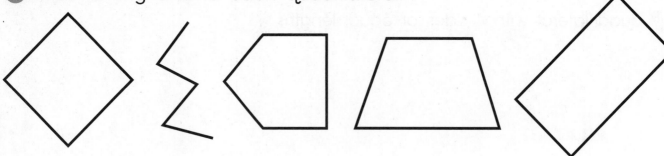

2 Draw a ring around each rhombus.

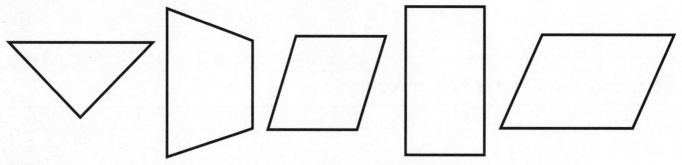

3 Cross out the figures that are NOT rectangles.

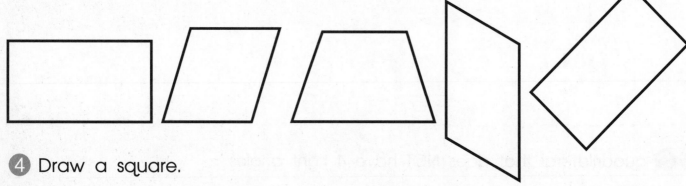

4 Draw a square.

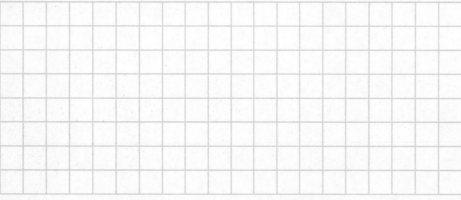

⭐ **Tell how a square is also a rectangle.**

Unit 23 • Mathematics Intervention Activities Grade 3 • © 2014 Newmark Learning, LLC